LET'S
UNDERSTAND
OUR**EXISTENCE**

LET'S UNDERSTAND OUR EXISTENCE

THE ANSWER TO YOUR INQUISITIVENESS

SUDHIR SINGHANI

PARTRIDGE

A Penguin Random House Company

To order additional copies of this book, contact
Partridge India
000 800 10062 62
www.partridgepublishing.com/india
orders.india@partridgepublishing.com

Introductory

Here the topic is about the 'life'; the story of the existence of human; from origin to today's so advance and modern way of living, 'the life' not only of man but of every creature and the story of the appearance, decent and evolution of man and all the existing living beings.

I am going to tell you, the idea that how I got inspiration to write about this thesis. Actually I am a person among the people who are just stream-lined and uni directed, who have got a very simple way of living, which is quite monotonous in which they think just for earning money for their living. Their routine, even thinking is so simple that whenever I talked them about something extra ordinary, like how the seasons change? How it rains? Why the earth moves? How far the stars will be and in what numbers in this eternal sky? How deep the oceans are? How man got his today's appearance, the shape and the body? Was there a miracle or a magic? How our body functions are finalized, Some what about the wonders of nature? Why do we live, after all, what is the aim of life? How many verities are there of the living creatures and how they got the existence? May there be life elsewhere in the universe? Then the behavior was noticed what non sense you are talking about? What do we have to do with all these, in what sense it is useful to us?

But by the course of time I thought, each of these questions have still not been answered, but what has been known still or has been found out by the science should be familiar to the common man, such as the above questions have been answered by recent discoveries of science, such as it is clear that the seasons and the day-night do change with the systematic movements of earth around the Sun in a parabolic pathway of the rotation and the revolving on its axis where the balancing of the force obtained by the big bang and the universal gravitation of a land mass, science has also measured the depth of the oceans where the maximum depth of the pacific ocean is near about 11 thousand meters and same as this, the maximum height of the topmost peak of a mountain is measured 8848 meters. As science explains what and how about the happening of any phenomenon, but we have to go through the enthusiasm begins with the questioner word WHY. So in this sequence I thought to put my ideas and views before the people, in the form of this thesis. Though we don't know every thing, but we may discuss about the topics to be taken for review. This thesis contains my knowledge, my views and collections from various points of my study, which are expressed before you, to be reviewed.

Here is the story of the struggle for the existence of the living world from the beginning to today's modern way of the struggle of life. Here I have used the word 'philosophy' because philosophy means to express own view after getting knowledge and experience of any subject on various basis with different logics.

There may be some criticism of my thesis that biology has been considered as a prominent way, for the idea here. But I would like to explain here that the subject is 'philosophical review of life'; "life" one of the most important words which means the way of living. So the only thing which gives the foundation for the study of life; where 'bio' means the living and 'logy' means study; so biology is the subject which studies the living world. As deep we think, we may plunge in the ocean of this controversial living world of explorer.

There may be many repetitions in various topics to explain the theme of the view. So finally, here; with expectations of your criticisms the logic begins.

Preface

I started writing a long ago but now I am to finalize it, as from several days I had a subject on which I want to express my opinion before you for review of yours. The subject is about the life. The life of not only man but also of every creature, after all human has been developed after crossing several stages from the ancestor species of those creatures. Here are some very common controversies of the living world and of the universe to be told and explained before you.

Here 'philosophy of life' means the basic criteria behind the life. There are several questions in human mind, which have still not been answered' like; WHAT is life? Who has created this world? Who generates and destroys the life, the livestock and the materialistic things? After all what is the aim of life? There is a question in my mind that the sky is unlimited but everything has its an end and edge, and in the sky there are billions and trillions of the stars, but they will also be in a limited quantity and where the availability of these stars is ended or exhausted, what begins there? So many questions like these often come in our mind, but we neglect these, because we have got no answer for those. It is quite natural. Here I have used the word 'NATURAL', which is commonly used where no answer is found but common people usually use 'THE GOD' on place of this word.

If there no answer is found, we say it was the will of god and he is the super powerful personality and what he only wants is occurred in this universe. I do say that there may be supernatural power which has created the world but it is the nature. The nature of any particle, of any material, or any atom is the primary symbolist property of this destructible (unstable) world. As there in chemistry it is supposed as natural that there is a particular charge upon an ion as positive or negative; then the syllabus of the subject begins with this supposition because there is no answer for the word 'natural'.

So here it is tried to explain that no one has got the answer to each of these questions but much more has been answered in recent discoveries which has been possible through the enthusiasm of the human mind so man should not think helpless and not to say it is the will of god but should satisfy his inquisitiveness. According to science, the origin of the universe, creation of the earth and development of the human and the prosperity of men has been the result of the experiments done by the nature. Nature has still been experimenting on all his universal things and after a few pride years we will see the results of these experiments. As we generally know that the man has been developed from monkeys [the ape] towards his modern individuality, [studies have shown that human DNA shows the 98.5%similarity with ape's genetic DNA] after the work of millions of years of the evolution and after a certain period we will see the quite different human from today's common man. All this will be the result, of nature's work on the natural world for a better tomorrow and for more efficiency in connection with the survival of the species in the new and changed circumstances. Here in case of Human being, the evolution and appearance of hands in past a few million years nearly 13, for more work to be done towards the creativity and to be 'constructive' and Human brain is so much developed in last a few thousand years to get more efficiency and to be 'Instructive' in a sequent but a spontaneous way according the circumstances appeared with the time.

After all the nature has got a beautiful world with new horizon by the help of the experiments accused on the universe but there are some limitations also to remain this world safe because as human has got the key board and the whip to tame and alter his surrounding things for his convenience could destroy the natural and systematic world and network of the living beings with the interference to this systematic nature. It has been tried to understand the world and the nature but the whole world too, in this thesis with the help of various topics.

Science has got much more about the origin and development of life that "how and when the life has begun and developed throughout various steps, but it has still not been answered that why this life is originated and by whom is inspired?" All of these questions have not been answered but what has been known still must be familiar to a common man. And man should be optimistic and identified with the theme and the triumph of life. The enthusiasm of human mind in a few recent years has given so many things invented such as aero planes, space satellites, various systems of technology i.e. internet, mobiles, televisions, cameras, various vehicles for convenience such as cars, trucks etc for transportations of people and goods. All these have made life much comfortable and convenient which happened just through understanding the nature and the natural things surround us and also the nature of each of the particle or the constituent of all the surrounding matter and the energy within it; even understanding the energy of an electron, a proton and a neutron have given so many sources of energy and revolutionary things for a much successful and prospered mankind which has been in just recent few thousand years.

About 4.6 billions years ago the earth was originated. First of all a hot and fast moving gaseous mass was condensed into a solid piece of this land mass and now it has got today's form which has become cooler and has got today's cool temperature, favorable for the origin and existence of the living world. How a long period of about 900 million years was spent by the Earth from the origin to get the first living being about 3.6 billion years back from today. The magma comes out we see when a volcano splits, shows that how hot the inner core of the earth is (there is up to 6600 degree Celsius temperature in the inner core of the Earth), but due to the decrease in atmospheric temperature the outer surface became cooler in a long period of millions of years. After various ups and downs, various times of raining and making the steam and after a long period of these changes, the life came to the earth into the water in the form of unicellular organism (the smallest living being, as in form of a single cell, the smallest unit of life; which consists of about one billionth part of a meter in size, got the activities of a living being.)These unicellular organisms converted into multi cellular after facing various temperatures, climatic and situational changes as favorable and adverse. And then after evolution in various stages today's creatures including all the varieties of the living beings we see today including human; the most advanced creature has gotten by the nature being as different branches of the living pedigree.

Here it has been tried to explain the natural phenomenon happening to the appearance existence and living of a common man but also to the existence and survival of all the living creatures. There are so many controversies among the people about the living world and the human existence, so many superstitions and fantasies are prevalent about the appearances and origin of human and the living world, which is quite natural because the Evolution is so gradual process that a common man can't understand it in a common way but a detailed study of years could only explain it and also due to the too short period of a human being which is about 60, 70 but not more then 100 years which is quite tiny with compared to the evolution of millions of years, it is also because the present view of the living world commonly seems eternal and without any fundamental changes.

About the origin of the universe, development of the earth, rising of life on this blue planet and the evolution of modern man, about human behavior as natural selection, about some philosophy of god, sexual behavior of other creatures as well as human, modern social status of man and the huge amount in millions of different variety of creatures and plants existing on each of the possible bit of our unique planet—all these topics are going to be discussed here with various logics.

"Philosophical Review of Life"

Always there; several questions stand in human mind about the existence, the existence of himself and of course of his surrounding nature. Here further scientific description of our living world is going to clarify about the nature and the mankind along with the other living world that how this entire network of living creatures of our planet got appearance and continues in all the possible regions of AIR, EARTH SURFACE and AQUA having so diverse and wonderful identity.

Here we are going to have a review of the existence of surrounding nature in a sequent and systematic manner where the scientific vision of the Universe and Earth is going to be visualized and the appearance and evolution of the living world, from the smallest living being as a virus or bacteria to the huge animals still known such as Dinosaurs including all the existing creatures along with human. The story of past 3.6 billion years of the living beings including the decent of human being that how and when the mankind could be developed and understanding the Diversity of living beings, Aim of being a living being, the theme behind the sexual behavior, also understanding the modern view of the social appearance of mankind. Great endless Universe, the Earth and its origin along with the origin and evolution of life, appearance and success of mankind, theme behind the variety of the living creatures surround us, Aim of life, the sexual behavior of human along with other creatures, social behavior of human being likewise various topics are going to be reviewed and being answered further.

1

The Great Endless Universe

*A*s it is well known that we live in a planet named the great earth which is a member of our solar system. In solar system there are nine planets like our earth and some of these have their own satellites too. All the planets rotate on their axis and revolve around the sun. Including all these our solar system is the part of our Galaxy 'The Milky Way'. There are various other solar systems in the galaxies like this and many of the other galaxies there in the entire universe. The universe is so huge that no one has been able to understand its horizon, and no where else the signs of life have been found. Not only all the masses available in the universe are totally movable but each of the atom as a constitution of any matter is also moving in any manner at all in a particular orbit sustained as its nature, due to flow and transformation of energy, because nothing is stable and eternal.

The universe has got billions and trillions of stars; some of them are also bigger than the Sun up to 800 times but man has still not *been able to find out the life on any other planet of our galaxy or another. It has been found out that no matter can travel faster than light and man has gone so far with the speed of light by the help of his scientific instruments but nowhere has got life. No one knows where the universe gets its end.* **There are billions of stars bigger than the sun available in the universe they have got more power and energy but they have no planet like earth. These stars are so far from us that the distance is measured in 'light year' where a light year is so called the distance traveled by the sunlight in a year and the sunlight goes with the speed of 3 hundred thousand kilometers in a second. So we can imagine that how far the other stars and galaxies are, what we can't understand the horizon of the universe in a common view.**

2

Origin of the Universe

In fact, the universe is so large that we have still got just a little knowledge about it. At present it looks like that all the Galaxies and stars going away from the center of the universe and the stars go away from the center of their galaxy. In this way the universe is going to extent itself; indicates the red shift found in the spectrum of the light which comes from the stars, the red shift means, the light is made of spectrum of 7 colors, in which red color band found in the light shows a shift in its frequency band with the time, which means the change in the position of the star. All this process of extend shows that there has been an explosion in a huge land mass and that land mass has been participated into various pieces of masses which have become the stars, planets comets and all these. This explosion theory is known as BIG BANG THEORY. Because of the explosive movement, all the masses got a speed and a pathway, came into attraction and repulsion towards each other and because of the balancing of the centripetal and centrifugal forces, masses got the movements around each-other ; attraction because of gravitation due to magnetic field created by the melt magma and the gases generating the electrical and magnetic field by blowing beneath the surface of any planet or land mass(the Universal Gravitation of any mass) and repulsion due to the force given by the explosion at the time of origin (Big Bang). Here the pathways of the planets and some other masses around the Sun or other stars and the natural satellites revolving around the planets such as the moon of Earth and the still known 14 moons means natural satellites of the biggest planet of our Solar system; Jupiter; could be understood by the method of today's artificial man made satellites launch systems where the centripetal force is given through the thrust of the different launch vehicles such as PSLV(POLAR SATELLITE LAUNCH VEHICLE) and GSLV(geostationary satellite launch vehicle) and the centrifugal force already existing as the universal gravitation of our planet Earth and when the satellite reaches in the path where the gravitation and the given force both becomes equal the satellite starts revolving in the same way of the natural planets and satellites. This process of rotations and revolving initiates towards the continuity as eternal due to the law of the motion given by sir Isaac Newton where a thing continues on its way if no force is enforced. Here, we are to discuss that how the explosion initiated the origin of the universe but by whom and how the matter was generated as basis of the explosion is still unknown?

All the pieces of mass in this universe are in momentum, every piece of land mass moves around its objective goal, such as various planets including our earth move around the sun with another movement of revolving on its axis. These planets have their own satellites revolving around them and the sun also revolves around the center of the galaxy and various other stars like sun also revolve around their galaxies center point. This revolving and rotating movement may be understood from a playing instrument called a **billet** (Lattoo). A **billet** is a round shaped playing instrument made of wood with a pointed tip of iron; which is thrown by a rope rounded around it. When we through it by pulling the rope rounded on it, the instrument starts rotating on it's tip and also revolves, if it is slightly bent and a simple harmonic motion starts. As we know that the earth is slightly bent about 23.5* from its axis, so this is the reason for the revolving of the earth around the sun. This billet shows the same momentum of the planets and is a very good example of the rotation and revolving movement. Here the initiating force is given through pulling the rope and in case of planets the basic force has been the explosion of the BIG BANG.

In this way 'all the elements existing in this universe rotate and revolve in hope of any revolution'. All the galaxies too revolve in their specified pathways. Entire universe is in an expansion and all the masses are being away from each other.

This universe is a question itself; where it has got its end and edge? Where it begins from? How many stars and galaxies it does have? None knows the answer of these questions and science has still not been able to find out. After-all, this universe is very beautiful and filled with wonders; man has to go through it and has to get the answers.

3

Origin of our Earth

Earth is a unique creation of nature. Science has still got about 110 types of elements existing in this entire universe constituting each and every atom or molecule of any matter. According to their properties these elements have been systematized in the periodic table and a proper utilization of these elements is being done for the convenience and prosperity of the mankind through

creating so many things being invented nowadays, such as different electronic devices, medical equipments and so many sectors useful in our routine and daily living such as Aviation, transporting etc. All these are not present from the olden time but are converted to their complex forms from the simple forms. The earth is not formed suddenly in a simple way or by magic of a miracle but after crossing various steps and a long duration of time, it has got its today's beautiful form.

We see the day from dawn to morning and from morning to evening and from evening to the night and again a morning continues towards the same routine. And we also see the days being changed from one to another and so on by crossing the routine life in these days we see seasons being changed from winter to summer from summer to rain and so on the repetitions from year to year. So there is no way for the stability and each of the moment is to change, this is called the LIFE. This conversion of day and night and the change of the seasons is due to the movements of Earth; where the rotating on it's axis results the day and night and the revolving of the Earth in a parabolic pathway around the sun makes the cause for the seasons from winter to summer and from summer to rain and again from rain to winter continuously. **During the revolving the earth comes near to the sun, which results increase in temperature in summer where the distance is about 147million kilometers and then evaporation of water in summer makes the clouds for the rain and through crossing the period of rain the earth reaches somewhat more distant from the sun, of a maximum distance of about 153 million kilometers then this difference of distance causes the winter with the decrease in the temperature. All this happens due to the parabolic pathway of the simple harmonic motion around the sun called the revolution of the earth.** *This distance of Earth which is approximate 150 million kilometers from the sun is the lowest distance from any star existing in the sky, other stars are millions and billions but also trillions of kilometers away from our Earth. These movements of the planets including Earth are same as the movements of man made satellites we use to send in recent time.*

About 4.5 to 4.6 billion years back the earth was originated, as it is proved by science by the methods developed, such as 'carbon dating' of any particle. Carbon dating is a method; in which an isotope of carbon molecule (eg.-C-14) shows a

particular period of degradation; so that we can specify the time of that matter by presence of this type of carbon in any matter, mostly this type of carbon is present simultaneously with a normal carbon. There are various controversies among the people about the origin of Earth; some people believe that this world is created by god as his special creation. It is considered that god has created this universe and regulates various phenomena on this earth.

An olden consideration says that this earth has taken birth as a piece separated from the sun. But modern scientist theory says that earth and the other planets of the solar system are generated from a very hot and fast moving round shaped gaseous mass; a ball of fire. This round ball converted into a solid mass after cooling a long time. This evidence took place about 4.5 to 5 billion years ago. At this stage earth had got heavy elements such as iron, nickel, sulfur, phosphorus etc., carbon was also a part of this mass. But till then the oxygen was not a part of this material. Heavier metals were in the core of the mass and outer layer was of lighter metals like silica and carbon. And all this was surrounded by gaseous substances. Because of the access heat more and more volcanoes used to blast at that time. This excessive heat created reactions among various elements and converted them from elements to substances. Ammonia and methane etc. gasses were formed from their elements respectively; nitrogen, hydrogen and carbon with hydrogen. After all this process of reactions, oxygen was formed, which reacted with hydrogen spontaneously and created water in the gaseous form but oxygen was not present in free as in molecular form yet. Then earth went cooler as this steam converted into water in accordance with the seasonal fluctuations; this cycle of steam to water and water to steam made the chances for the earth to become cooler. Then the oceans were created and with the disturbance to the land mass the continents and mountains were formed. All this process took a vast period of time, about millions of years. This process of becoming cool from so hot temperature may be proven by the volcanoes splitting out on different places on the Earth where the inner core of Earth has been known up to about 6600 degrees Celsius temperature having in it and the outer surface has been cooler to the normal well known temperature from some minus degrees to near to 50-60 degrees in Celsius.

4

Origin and Evolution of Life

Amino Acid

Nature has created all the living creatures in his laboratory; not as a miracle or a magic but gradually after keen efforts accused on its nature, since a long period of time about 3.6billion years. "In these efforts nature has got the human; as its greatest invention and now the nature has tried to make the man as macro man by developing of brain and two hands with power to control the overall world, in his laboratory".

All the things we see around in living form, from where and how did they come from? Were all these things present here since this earth originated? Or have been created with a magic or a miracle? No, according to various evidences, it has been proven that these various varieties of living creatures are generated step by step. First of all the simplest and smallest form of life (creature) was born in the form of unicellular organism. Then these smallest and simple living creatures are generated step by step. First of all the simplest and smallest form of life (creature) was born in the form of unicellular organism. Then these smallest and simple living beings converted into the bigger and complex living beings through millions of generations through adapting different activities and abilities to conquer the struggle for keep living. **This process of Evolution from simple to the complex could be understood by the process of generating or producing process of any living being such as a human, an animal or a plant. We see that a small seed of a particular plant can produce a new plant in favorable conditions but of its own pedigree, same in the production process of a human being also a micro and tiny ova with a micro sperm initiates producing a new fetus and then this fetus matures up to a new human being. So it is clear that the entire existing living creatures are born through the system from simple and micro to the complex and so huge personality.** *As far as we know the species existing on the entire earth are just about one percent of the species disappeared yet, in this consequence of the experiments accused by the nature. What the existing species we see today is the achievement of the nature in past millions of years with the law of '***Survival of the fittest'*** discovered by the great philosopher **Charles Darwin**. The existing creatures we see around us have conquered the struggle in the battle of the living world. In this connection, I would like to discuss here that we know that some generations back about 2 or 3 generations, people used to deliver a big number of children as 8, 9, 12 but a few of them used to survive, this was because of the struggle for the existence. So many reasons were there for the high mortality rate; such as diseases, starvation, flood, draught, pathogenic micro organisms, unavailability of medicines and so on a few means 2 or 3 children could only continue the generation and man was to live same as the other living creatures due to not understanding the nature. The only law "survival of the fittest" was there to continue the human race.*

It is said mythological that the life is specially created by the god. In Hinduism it is said that '"Brahma"—the god of creativity', himself by his various organs has created the world; it is believed that the birds from—chest, goats from mouth, trees and plants from the tentacles of the body and human was generated from his head. Here a question arises that the god is also imagined in the form of a human having a head, chest and the tentacles, how these imaginations are possible before the appearance of the human race. Another myth about the origin of the living world in "Bible" it is said that god created this world in just 6 days in various steps. All these mythological aspects are just imaginary and are only based on the stories written by some authors in the olden times. These myths are so much spread and fulfilled because in those times the population was too little and people were in dark about the nature and science; this type of literature was 'a line of stones' or a ray of light in the dark so that they followed them without understanding, but the only theory which has been proven by experiments and evidences is the "Bio chemical evolution" theory.

According this theory, origin of life began in the ocean about 3.5 to 3.6 billion years ago (there are evidences for the actual time;—a blue green algae, a type of algae, named Barbartonensis still found floating on the surface of some particular oceans having DNA about 3.2 billion years old) When simple elements reacted each-other and converted into complex substances. In these reactions a revolution occurred when first molecule of DNA was generated; the actual soul of a living phenomena. For this substance-production the energy was received from ultra violet rays coming from the sun, electrical emission of lightening, high temperature of the volcanoes and radio activity existing in the substances of the earth etc. As the favorable conditions occurred, this DNA with another constituting element of any living body; the 'protein' molecules and other complex chemical substances ;the first organization with DNA surrounded with protein molecules was formed but it was without life, an imaginary titled the 'pre-life constitution'. These pre-life constitutions got the signs of life gradually followed the qualities of life later. This happened about 3.5 to 3.6 billion years ago. From these pre-life constitutions; the proto viruses (the smallest and primary form of viruses with a strand of DNA in a protein envelop; can replicate, multiply or regenerate in just any other living body or a culture media with abundance of organic substances), viruses (all the pathogenic living bodies even smaller then the bacteria having the sign of life in any other living body), prokaryotes (primary true living beings with single cell as complete body within it such as protozoa's e.g. amoeba, euglena etc.) and then eukaryotes(multi-cellular organisms) were born. It was a gradual evolution. Up to 2.5 billion years the life was beneath the oceanic surface and about 1 billion years ago from today the first amphibians(creatures living in both the water and on land) began to develop and the living beings now started coming towards the land and a new horizon was to be achieved in the living world.

The origin and evolution of life can be explained in these two major steps-first the Chemical evolution and secondly Biological or Organic evolution.

CHEMICAL EVOLUTION:—

From the origin of the earth to creation of the primary organism, there are various steps in chemical evolution—

Origin of primitive earth and atmosphere:—

No one surely knows that how this earth came to its existence and who created it? According to old myths Earth took birth as a piece separated from the sun. But modern thought says that the earth and the other planets were generated from a very hot and a circulating gaseous ball. Gradually it became cooler and solid accordance with time. This ball had got iron, nickel, copper, sulfur, phosphorus, along with carbon. And so on the earth was created in various layers as the inner layer was hotter; couldn't become cool and the outer layer became cooler with the atmospheric temperature. Due to the hot inner layer more and more volcanoes were used to split.

Because of excessive heat carbon reacted with other elements and produced carbides which are the main constituents of earth's crust even today. Reacting to each-other and in mutant (convertible) circumstances other elements and compounds like ammonia, nitrogen, hydrogen, methane etc. were created. As methane was created from carbon and hydrogen, ammonia from nitrogen and hydrogen, and so on hydrogen reacted to oxygen but due to hyper activity of oxygen and very high temperature; oxygen couldn't be free in molecular form and reacted with other elements; generated steam. In this consequence because of cooling the earth steam converted into water and rained later and so on the oceans were taken place.

Origin of simple compounds

Hydrogen was the most active element in all the available substances. Because of this activity and due to the energy of ultra violet rays hydrogen reacted with carbon and nitrogen and resulted into the ammonia methane, ethane and propane etc various compound substances. Other organic compounds essential for life; such as fatty acids, glucose, amino acids, nitrogenous bases were formed in various gradual steps from these basic substances.

As long as temperature of earth went down, steam converted into water and water formed steam due to the solar energy. So it rained time to time, and then some water stored in various places which were submerged and in this way oceans, lakes, rivers etc. were formed. Some parts of surface of the earth came up because of excessive heat and some remain immerged. At that time earth quacks, volcanoes flood, and various disaster type incidents were in progress. These phenomena were a large source of energy at the primitive circumstances of the earth.

Formation of the complex compounds

All the process of formation of various simple and complex organic compounds was continue in the water. Gradually when the temperature of the surface decreased up to 100 *C and hydrogen reacted and created various hydrocarbons. Metal carbides reacted with water and created other hydrocarbons (carbon + hydrogen). And so on hydrocarbons reacted with steam and created various other carbohydrates (organic compounds with carbon+ hydrogen+ oxygen) like acetaldehydes having oxygen with hydrocarbon.

Hydrocarbons, its' derivatives, ammonia, water and other substances formed various other complex compounds as carbohydrates, fats, fatty acids, amino acids and proteins etc. by the process of condensation, polymerization, oxidation and reduction etc. The energy source for these processes was ultra violet rays, radiations, lighting, and volcanoes etc.

Just at the same time Purin and pirimidin the nitrogenous bases (the two basic and essential parts of DNA constitution; the informatics and controller unit of any cell) were generated by various chemical reactions. Many compounds essential for life in creatures were generated at that time. All this process of generating organic compounds was continue in water so this solution may be called as "pre-biotic soup". In this pre-biotic soup simple compounds condensed and produced more complex compounds like fats, proteins, polysaccharides, nucleosides and nucleotides; the constructing units *of DNA, Carbohydrates and fats produced at that time are the part of today's living beings and are the source of energy. The units of amino acid condensed and produced a chain of poly peptides which is the protein; the structure of any vital organism. In fact this word organism is meant itself, an organization of carbon compounds, where organ is a regional name of carbon. The invention of protein was the first important phenomenon for the creation of life, and the second was that Phosphoric acid, sugars, and nitrogenous bases created nucleic acids (DNA).*

Because of this condensation tendency nucleic acid and protein condensed into nucleoprotein some other complex compounds like this such as glyco-lipid (fat with glucose), chromo lipid were created in the pre biotic soup. All these compounds are the first responsible and organizers of the body of any living being.

The above description of creation of complex substances is not just imaginary but scientifically proven with the help of different experiments accused by a lot of scientists time to time. An experiment showing the condensation of simple compounds such as methane, ammonia, steam and formation of complex compounds such as polypeptides, polysaccharides, carbohydrates, different types of protein molecules fats, fatty acids which are the basic constituents of any living body, generated in the laboratory was awarded by the Noble prize to the scientists; Miller and yore. The energy source was taken as electrical emission as lightening and the substances were kept for a long period in those circumstances for about 7 days and the pre biotic soup was obtained. The same circumstances were generated as would have been during the initiation of the living phenomenon on the earth in the olden times.

Another experiment showed by Dr. Hargovind Khorana an America based scientist who was awarded with Noble prize in 1968, declared the possibility of full living being which could be created in a laboratory; at Wisconsin university of America, produced a DNA molecule in lab. And by this he put the world into a great wonder. It means the substances and complex compound elements present today are generated from simple compounds with the help of energy obtained from different sources.

BIOLOGICAL OR ORGANIC EVOLUTION

Biological means the evolution from the non-living substances to living, the gradual and sequent development from simple organisms to the complex.

Gradually in the pre biotic soup, the molecules of protein attracted towards each other and reacted; created a chain like structure. These big protein molecules had ionic charge and because of this charge various water molecules stick around these big protein molecules. These big colloidal molecules were called "micro spheres", and group of these micro spheres were the first living molecules, having pre life verifications and were so called the "pre-life constitutions. These pre-life constitutions are the middle stage between non-living and living beings; and so on after some changes these molecules got the characteristics of a living being.

FORMATION OF FIRST LIVING BEING

When the temperature of the atmosphere decreased up to about 80* to 70*C and became favorable for the living phenomenon after a certain period, the greatest event took birth on the unique earth to initiate the revolution to start the evolution of life. It happened about 3.5 billion years ago.

Pre-life constitutions were the structure having protein surrounded by the coating of fatty acids. This coating of fatty acids was with ionic charge on it. The ionic charge condensed water molecules surround the structure. Because of the inter-action of the inner molecules and also with the surrounding organic substances the structure collected on the outer layer and created the covering of the inner molecules as so called membrane could be named plasma membrane. And then so many anabolic (constructive) and catabolic (destructive) reactions started in the organization of these 'pre-life constitutions'. Some proteins produced in these reactions started working as various types of enzymes, caused the reactions much faster as metabolic and produced a lot of energy to initiate the vital activities of the structure to be rewarded as a living phenomenon.

The energy source for these reactions was the organic substances and these substances were taken from the surrounding-water;

the process was same as in the fermentation where a glucose molecule produces ethanol and a lot of energy. In this way the 'pre life constitutions' changed into anaerobic heterotrophic phenomena (without taking oxygen and getting nutrients from surrounding). The structure went increasing in size and shape because of absorbing substances from the surroundings and then started dividing into pieces. And so on they got multiplicity and finally called reproduction.

Till then the nucleic acids (RNA and DNA) were produced. So because of having the capacity of replication or multiplicity, these started dividing; with the abundance of energizing substances; means nutritional substances' started growing and multiply in numbers. This process started continuing multiple times' and the story began of the existence, the existence of the living world in the smallest and the micro way. Here the presence of DNA or RNA was the basic revolution for the living world because it had the two basic transforming characters; first was to replicate and create the copies of the original one and the second was to synthesize the RNA to produce the protein molecules; the structural substance of a living being with the basic characters of the living phenomenon by transcription of the codes integrated within the DNA. It means the molecules of DNA and RNA can be compared with today's virus (we generally listen this word from doctors as viral fever, viral infections etc deceases caused by virus is the same, present in the atmosphere since the origin of the living beings); which starts multiplying at entering any living cell, where it gets the organic substances as nutrition. As we know the DNA molecule has got the efficiency of carrying genetic information may be compared with "gene"; were in a very tiny form as in small nucleotide at the time of origin. These nucleotide small chains connected each other and created the nucleic acids. And then fortunately protein was coated around the nucleic acids and created the primary viruses, which are also present today. In this way the first life came to the earth in the form of a virus.

Anaerobic (not taking oxygen) Heterotrophic (taking nutrition from outside) structure having nucleic acid (DNA) was the first organized cell of the earth, which was like a prokaryotic (primary type of cell with limited organelles within it and also without a nucleus) bacteria of Kingdom Monera (a group of tiny organisms with some basic similar characters specified in the classification of the living animals). And *then from these prokaryotic Monera organisms, other cells named Protista (having nucleus) were produced in which nucleic acids (DNA) were present in groups in the nucleus(the central part of the cell). The most important thing here is that from virus, prokaryotes and then eukaryotes were produced and both prokaryotes and eukaryotes were "Heterotrophy" and obtained nutrient substances from the surrounding but couldn't produce nutrients themselves. Still the living body was dependent on the surrounding substances and called heterotrophy. In this way, at beginning the life started the mode to get the nutrients for energy from the organic substances available in the surrounding and accepted heterotrophy. But now as we know various types of nutrition such as autotrophy; means to produce nutrients itself with the help of sunlight etc. But at the beginning the living beings got energy through the only mode of nutrition from the surrounding as HETEROTROPHY.*

Origin of Auto tropism (first system of self generating nutritional substances such as photosynthesis)

Till that time only anaerobic hetero tropes used available organic substances and increased in numbers, this process went up-to millions of years. Then as gradually the organic food material (the natural food source) was finished, other process for nutrition, to get energy was adapted and developed; these anaerobic HETEROTROPHS started using inorganic substances for energy as food material (nutrients) and produced organic substances. It was the first step of auto tropism. These hetero tropes used anaerobic reduction (in brief: reduce the hydrogen atom from any substance) for getting energy because they could not use solar energy in the absence of chlorophyll (the green pigment of the plants responsible for production of the organic substances as nutrients with the help of solar energy). In this way in the case of autotrophy, Chemo-autotrophy was the first source of energy. Today also this Chemo-autotrophy method can be seen in sulfur-bacteria in the deep of the ocean. This bacteria intakes, Hydrogen Sulfide (H_2S) along with carbon dioxide and produces glucose ($C_6H_{12}O_6$) and sulfur with lots of energy. This process is same as in the plants where the photosynthesis process produces glucose and release oxygen on place of sulfur.

The chemical energy became insufficient for all type of primary organisms such as bacteria. Some of the sulfur-bacteria reached to the sea-surface, where another way of energy source was to be discovered. Then another stage of evolution was invented by the nature in which a small form of chlorophyll as Bacterial-chlorophyll named PORPHIRIN having no Magnesium (which is present in true chlorophyll) was generated to the bacteria of that time. In these bacteria's there was a capacity of using solar energy in order to get food. This was the second method of Auto tropism, photo synthetic autotrophy. This type of autotrophy can be seen even today, in sulfur bacteria lying on the sea surface. This type of chlorophyll used sulfur compounds to produce organic substances as nutrition for the structure of its own.

Till that time there was no oxygen present on the earth in independent form. The process of mutation changed the bacterial-chlorophyll into true chlorophyll by sudden changes in the genes and included the magnesium molecule to the chlorophyll. Then this true chlorophyll used water molecules (H_2O) on place of hydrogen sulfide (H_2S) and in spite of liberating sulfur it liberated oxygen (O_2) and this process was same as today's "photosynthesis-process". In this way Chemo-synthetic Prokaryotic cell changed into photo-synthetic autotrophic cell; which can be compared with today's blue green algae. In 1968 a blue green algae named 'Archaeospheraids Barbartonensis" was discovered and was about 3.2 billion years old. So it certifies that at that time living beings like blue green algae were present on this earth but in the oceanic water. So this preliminary process of PHOTOSYNTHESIS resulted into a big revolution for the evolution and diversity of the living creatures of that time towards the new Era by getting more energy by oxidizing the nutritional substances more effectively.

Oxygen Revolution

Oxygen was not present already since the birth of the earth but it was generated by the evolution of photo-synthetic process. At that time oxygen liberation to the surrounding by this process of photo-synthesis was a great revolution for the evolution and development of ancient living beings and for the changes in the surrounding atmosphere. At that time production of oxygen

created great and important changes on the earth. *The basic changes which affected the evolution of the living world of that time and gave a route to them may be discussed as under:—*

1   *By liberation of Oxygen the media of atmosphere changed to oxidizing form, so more chemical evolutionary chances were over.*

2   **With this oxygen a layer, about 15 miles above the earth surface was created named OZON LAYER. So the ultra violet rays; harmful for the living beings, coming towards the earth from the sun were now stopped so a new way was opened for the aquatic life to launch at the earth's territory.**

3   **Oxygen reacted with Methane and produced Carbon dioxide which was essential for photosynthesis and so on also reacted with Ammonia and liberated Nitrogen which gave a speed to the evolution of life because Nitrogen is an important part of the protein structure, the main element of our body structure and also the basic element of the enzymes, which gives the speed to any chemical reaction.**

In this way as the Oxygen liberated from the compounds it started a revolution in the evolution of the living world existing on that time and changed the way of nutrition and now a new era of living world was to be followed. Yet the hetero-tropes (creatures getting nutritional substances from surrounding) were present in the oceanic water and a simple and primary way of getting energy was in progress. This oxygen now started oxidizing the nutritional supplements and produced a lot of more energy. Here oxidizing means the burning of any matter because no matter can burn without oxygen.

Origin of True nucleus or eukaryotic cells:—

Oxy-respiration started with the production of free oxygen by this process living system, got 20 % more energy than before. Till then only prokaryotic cells (primary and simple cells) were present with limited and primary organelles. And so on to utilize more oxygen and to get more energy these prokaryotic cells converted into eukaryotic cells with true nuclei, Mitochondria and other cell organelles much developed with the time after the evolution in some generations. In this way after millions of years Eukaryotic unicellular organisms got existence in the oceanic aqua. This Eukaryotic Unicellular Organism was originated about 1.5 Billion years ago. These Eukaryotic unicellular organisms were just same as today's eukaryotic unicellular organisms, e.g. all the pathogenic Bacteria, Amoeba, paramecium etc micro organisms, what we hear about but can not see from the common eye. So it represents that all these micro organisms existing today have been the generations of those organisms developed at those times about 1.5 billion years back. In this way Eukaryotic unicellular organisms were created by "Gene—Mutation" and evolutionary effect from Prokaryotic cells. In these atmospheric effects the atmospheric changes as availability of nutritional supplements, surrounding temperature etc. were the most important effects.

Here it is important to understand a cell; cell is the smallest unit of any organism such as a house is built with the combination of bricks as its units; in this way a great combination of such small brick units makes o great construction. Cell is an individual and self controlled unit in about 1 billionth part of a meter in size. *There are two types of cells Prokaryotic and Eukaryotic. Prokaryotic cells were the primary and simple structural cells which were firstly present on this earth and came first; but the eukaryotic cells developed from these prokaryotic cells by having well developed organelles for utilizing more natural resources and more oxygen, so the eukaryotic cells were the complex organisms. All the creatures we see today, including us are having the structure of eukaryotic cells means well planned and complex eukaryotic cells.* **There are billions of cells within our body but developed from just a single cell during the development of a fetus. All the creatures we see are having billions of cells and called multi-cellular but are used to be developed from single a cell since the initiation of the fetus towards the birth of an infant.**

In this way creatures seen in this nature were not present already since the olden times but there was no life on the earth. By the chemical evolution process the first living creature was born. After this, because of the atmospheric changes it got adaptations and variations and that simple creature became the complex one by the atmospheric effect and changes of billions of years resulted in the descendants with some differences due

to the mutations in the generating genes of the ancestors. The complex creatures seen today are the result of environmental effects and adaptations acquired to fight with the un-favors of the surrounding atmosphere being as different branches of the ancestor living beings with the time.

Organic Evolution is the process in which, complex living beings are generated from simple living organisms by a long duration of time about thousands and millions of years in keen gradual and step by step changes, environmental changes played a great roll in these adaptations. Evolution is a continuous process going un-interrupted but keen gradual so we can't judge through our common observation. Even today the process of evolution is continue and in progress in each of the living being. In this evolution new species are developed when a generation differs in more characters from the generating species. By various evidences it is discovered that the ancient human being was bigger in size and powerful in physical ability but by environmental changes he lost his physical capability and came into today's form. If this gradual evolution continues till million years man may be changed into a new species but we will not be the witness till then and those existing people could also not be able to observe the changes because the olden; means our generation would have been disappeared till then.

Reasons for the environmental changes:—

The environmental changes are the result of the various activities of our surrounding atmosphere. First of all the universe is being extent so in this consequence the earth is being gradually cooler then the olden time. The two movements of our earth; rotating on it's axis and revolving around the sun, creates seasons and the day and night. Rain tides and lightening have played a great roll in the evolution of life. All these are the preliminary reasons for the environmental changes.

Ultra violet rays played a great roll for the energy as a first source from the sun. These uv-rays were the great cause of mutation (mutation means sudden changes in the DNA or Chromosomes resulting as the changes in the character or structure; to change one species to another). There are billions of varieties of living creatures, can be distinguished with each other because of having a lot of variations, in fact we can not imagine similarity or uniformity in these species but all these have some cardinal uniformities in organization and their biological activities. This uniformity represents the relation of all the creatures where it may be said that these living organisms are developed from the same ancestors a long ago. The similarities seen in the living being as common are as under:—

All the creatures take energy, nutrients from the surroundings. All the living beings multiply and reproduce. Transformation of hereditary characters and process of protein synthesis is same in all the living beings. All the living beings have the only genetic material DNA. All the living organisms look quite different from each other but have been developed till today's existence from a same fore-father.

In this entire world, the living beings seen in various different activities have reached today's individuality after a keen gradual process. There has been a specific time for the development of a particular creature. Scientists have developed a scale for the time of origin of earth and evolution of life which is divided into various channels named "GEOLOGICAL TIME SCALE"

According to geological time scale the age of earth is measured with various methods; up to 4.5 billion years. First of all a fast moving gaseous fire ball was there but cooled gradually and became a solid mass there were no chances for the life because of the too much high temperature and this period went up to about 900 million years. This period was called AZOIC ERA (non living age).

Then about 3.6 billion years back the age of living beings started when the first living organism split in the oceanic aqua. After that the time period is divided into 5 living eras of time. There have been great revolutions for these eras of time. These revolutions have been the cause for the change the stages of creature behavior, activities and variations etc. These revolutions can be compared with the disasters of different times. These are called geological revolutions. These geological revolutions were so effective that the mountains could change into oceans and some part of the oceans might become mountain and hills; a good example of these changes has been seen recently in the basin of Himalayas where some fossils have been found of aquatic animals existing millions years back which clarifies that there was an ocean, where the hills of Himalayas are today. The five eras according to Geological measurement of time of the living beings are:—

A. *Archeozoic era: 3.6 billion years back from today, period went about 2 billion years (Single cell living beings; from Viruses to micro bacteria, still single cell units couldn't become multi cellular up to 2 billion years)*

B. *Proterozoic era: 1.6 billion years back, for about 1 billion years (small delicate creatures of oceanic aqua without back bone and with a little developed nervous system and many more single cell living beings prospered but life was beneath the oceanic aqua)*

C. *Paleozoic era: 600 million years back, spent about 370 million years (small delicate animals like starfish, octopus and preliminary fishes etc were developed and prospered and the first animals with bones could now develop and later the plants and animals started coming out from the aqua to the terrestrial surface)*

D. *Mesozoic era: 230 million years back, period about 160 million years (Age of Reptilians including the huge Dinosaurs)*

E. *Cenozoic era: 70 million years back, still going on called the age of mammals (having mammary glands; feeding milk to the infants)*

So let's understand these eras with description—

*A. Archeozoic Era (**Archeo means oldest and zoic means living**):—After having no life earth spent about 900 million years and **about 3600 million years ago from today, a new era took place in the process of a gradual progress of time and nature, when the first living organism took birth in the form of a virus and developed up to the period of about 2 billion years and prospered up to the simplest true living organisms such as bacteria and blue green algae with a well developed nucleus means the life was just in the form of a single cell yet within the size of about 1 billionth part of a meter. So we can imagine how a long period 0f about 2 billion years took to form a true living organism. This was not a magic or a miracle but the efforts of the nature in his laboratory accused on the first living being and its descendent generations to adopt the surrounding atmosphere and nutrients to grow and reproduce from time to time, with the law given by Charles Darwin 'survival of the fittest as natural selection'***

B. Proterozoic era:—About 1.6 billion years ago geological revolution appeared due to the volcanoes and other activities of the earthen movements are so called the first geological revolution. And with this, the new era protierozoic started for about 1 billion years.

Yet the life was under water and the aquatic creatures were developed up to superior level and acquired the monopoly of the living world but the signs of creatures like today's existence were still not there. The creatures without back bone called non-chordates were prospered in this era in which the primary micro organisms like "protozoa" the single cell creatures, "coelenterate" (having a simple gut inside the body) "Arthropods"(having jointed legs like prawns) and "Annelids" like Earthworms type primary creatures with a little developed nervous system but not the brain were prospered up to this era about 600 million years ago. Blue green algae and bacteria were already existing multiplying in their generations but some other type of algae and fungus were developed with the adaptations acquired with the generations from time to time according to the surrounding circumstances of weather and availability and abundance of nutritional substances required for their living activities.

C. Paleozoic Era:—About 600 million years back when the second great geological revolution occurred, the new era began. This era was prospered up to 360 million years. This era was much more important for the biological evolution of the living creatures because the life was still under water before this era. Various non-chordates means without the spinal chord and bones were prospered eg.-Starfish, pearls oysters, octopus etc. type delicate creatures called mollusks were prevalent and without bones in their body. Now the animals and plants started coming out from the oceanic water to the terrestrial surface. Gradually the chordates (having bones) started originating in this era with the help of the evolution and the new characters adapted in the species and transferred these characters in the forthcoming generation; developed a new species which were fit for the survival in the new climate and atmosphere; those species which were not capable to adapt disappeared. Now the preliminary fishes started being developed and prospered up to a large variety with the characters adapted in different regions in the oceans of different climate as different temperature and different availability of specific nutrients.

The life was underwater still but in this era it started coming out from the aqua to the territory which was still infertile and without a living phenomenon. Here we can imagine that how a huge period of time about 3250 million years was spent to be capable for the terrestrial existence means just 250 million years back from today; the first creature appeared on the earth, which is a very little period in compared with the aquatic struggle of the living world. So from these fishes; the first amphibian (animals living in both water and terrestrial region like frog etc.) came to existence accordance with time and new characters adapted for survival. There are so many similarities in the aquatic and the amphibians which show the life coming out of the water. The development from the mollusks (aquatic delicate creatures without bones, living in shells) towards the fishes with gills and then from these fishes towards some varieties of pulmonary (lungs) fishes and then the amphibians show the gradual evolution from water to terrestrial. Then finally in this era some primary rubbing animals like snake named Reptilians started developing from the amphibians.

This is the tendency in any of the living being to adapt the necessary characters which are essential in the new atmosphere and the rest useless characters are disappeared with the time; this is a keen gradual process that we can not specify in a common observation but a thorough study can explain this process; for example, a man do exercise regularly or works more physically, get strong muscles developed, in the process of evolution this type of characters are transferred from generation to generation. It means the descendent generation of this man probably be strong in physical work with much developed muscles. In this way these type of characters acquired from the circumstances are transferred from generation to generation and if so many characters are acquired and developed in many generations a new species get developed with a long period of time in hundreds and thousands years; so the human also has been the result of about some millions of years to develop from the monkey world fore fathers. So many generations are being spent then a new species is developed after getting a lot of new characters developed according to the requirement of that time climate for food, shelter and safety. We can not judge that how the new variety of the living beings appeared, what we see around us. Our scientists with enthusiasm have discovered the laws of the *nature and made a great study on the fossils of the creatures found, have been the evidences for this evolution of the appearance of the various species developed from several other, in a manner of "simple to the complex'. In this consequence of evolution the ancestor living being re-produces same living beings as the descendents but after some generations some or one of the descendents appears as a quite different organism apart from the original one with some new characters and so a new species starts along with the original ancestors.*

Even the plants we see on earth were also got existence from the aquatic algae and developed up to the first terrestrial plant. Some type of primary auto synthetic plants with easier constitution like Mosses, ferns were mostly prospered on the territory of that primitive situation of the plants kingdom. The flowering plants seen mostly today were still not appeared but the plants such as coconut, palm and pine type conifer plants named as Gymnosperms were prospered and wide spread everywhere in this era about 230 million years ago. So we can imagine how a huge period of time spent for the appearance of today's living world.

D. Mesozoic Era : The middle age of the living world:—

About 230 million years back a revolution named Appalachian revolution Occurred on this earth's environment; due to the movements of the earth's crust and the magma insight it and the climate was totally changed some parts of the new mountains appeared and some peaks of them disappeared and submerged in the oceanic aqua. So in this new atmosphere some species adapted some new characters to survive and when more and more new characters were adapted some new species got appearance as the descendent generations of the ancestors. So the new species started coming up; which were capable to conquer the new climate with more difficulties, rest which species could not change or adapt themselves got disappeared and distinct. Some of the species of the ancestor generation continued in the original form and some new species with quite different qualities got existence. The period of this Mesozoic Era went up to about 160 million years. This Era is famous for its Reptiles and also called the "Age of Reptilians" Because of the monopoly of the reptiles like Dinosaurs. So many types of Dinosaurs were appeared in this era from their ancestor species in so gradual manner and in a long duration of time about 100 million years. It was not a miracle to introduce the species of those Dinosaurs but these were developed from their small sub species of their order; like the common lizards chameleons crocodiles and monitors etc.. In fact, at the beginning of this era the creatures of this reptilian family were with small body but as some of the species got conditions of the atmosphere too much favorable and the nutrients were in abundance due to the increase in the vegetation in a large amount, started growing in size. The plants appeared at that time were prospered in a large quantity and wide spread on every bit of the land as they got the favorable conditions to survive. In this way, the abundance of the vegetation inspired the small animals of reptilians and then the wide range of the dinosaurs was prospered. This era was prospered with Reptilians developed up to their apex of development but the animals called mammals (having mammary glands; feeding capacity) now began to appear and the first ovulating(egg lying) mammal took birth.

*This Mesozoic Era is divided into three steps of development; the first is Triassic, second one Jurassic and then the latest of this era Cretaceous. The Jurassic Era is most popular for the Dinosaurs with enormous personality, spent a long period of about 100 million years which is beyond the imagination. But in the next step cretaceous of the Mesozoic Era gave the decline of the Dinosaurs in lack of vegetation and due to some other inverted climate conditions. The reason for these inverted climate circumstances has been found that a huge meteoroid from space came towards the earth in a drastic speed and collided. In this collision a very big explosion with a great energy of more than some hydrogen bombs occurred. In this explosion so many clouds of dust occurred in the atmosphere for some years. A big amount of vegetation could not survive in absence of sunlight. So the animals with small body could get the nutrients and some who adapted themselves to enter in the oceanic water or deeper in soil to get nutrients, could survive further. So the huge personality Dinosaurs started disappearing due to starvation and not breathable atmosphere. **So in search of food and nutrients and fresh air to breath, the small reptilians started entering in the air and the first modern bird was taken birth. A fossil has been found some years ago which shows the characters of both the reptiles and the birds, scales on body like reptiles and feathers developed as birds and some other characters also show the***

appearance of birds from the snake or other reptile family named AECHEOPTERIS.

In this cretaceous period as the conditions of atmosphere improved the mammals started entering various atmospheres. The plants of primary level named Gymnosperm (having no flowers) and less developed plants were prospered in this Mesozoic era. The modern Angiosperms the true flowering plants started developing now as the circumstances appeared.

E. Cenozoic Era (Modern Era:—Age of Mammals)

It is also known as the "Modern Era". It started about 63 million years ago and still in progress. The imperialism of mammals and in plants; Angiosperms the modern flowering plants are prominently prospered in this Era.

According to the Geological time Scale the Cenozoic Era is divided into two major steps Tertiary and Quaternary. In Tertiary period the olden feeding animal called mammals from insectivores to carnivores (flesh eating) were developed. This period went up to about 62 million years. It was the time till no signs of human or the ancestor species of man were appeared. This Tertiary period was the time of prosperity of the mammals of modern age we see today commonly in our surrounding like camel, elephant, horse, monkey, apes etc. This was the period of the abundance of the vegetation and prosperity of the modern flowering plants and the chances for variations and prosperity of vegetation of new world as the nutrients were available for the animals. **This was the time when the early man started originating and started the revolutionary Bipedal movement and started the utilization of brain. The most important milestone was to be discovered now.**

The Quaternary period has been the period for the development of the modern man and some other mammals seen today. This Quaternary period is being so called since 1million years (10 lac) till today. The man has become superior among all the creatures because of the development of the brain and the two hands on spite of being forelimbs.

As Cenozoic era was divided into two periods' tertiary and quaternary, the primary time of quaternary period was the age of ice. And so on the creatures which could not bear the coldness disappeared, gradually. In this period about 400 thousand years back *from today the life of man started being social when man started utilizing the BRAIN, so this period was called the "age of man". Just in this period the delicate herbs like plants were developed and monocot plants (having single a part of seed) like maize got the topmost position in the world of plants.*

There had been a great Geological revolution after the Mesozoic era named as "Rock mountain revolution". During this revolution the 'Himalaya', Alps and Andes etc mountains were appeared due to the enormous effect of the magma beneath the Earth came out in the form of volcanoes and then the modern Cenozoic era was occurred.

So this was the great journey from the Chemical evolution to the today's form of biological evolution; and also the development of the most advanced true beast the HUMAN BEING.

In this way nature has got all the varieties of various creatures not in just a particular time or by a miracle of any magic, but it is the result of the hard work of millions of years by the nature in his laboratory the EARTH and nature is always continue with the experiments on it's creation and all the existing living phenomena and still is in search of better world with more efficiency and for the existence of the surviving species.

5

Appearance and Evolution of Human Being

(How man got his today's form)

*T*he evolution (here evolution means carrying the particular characters adapted in one generation; to the forthcoming races) of all the living beings has developed the complex creatures from the simple creatures. Just like the other animals the development of human has taken place from the simple to the complex because of the creation of the necessary characters' As we know human is a mammal (having mammary glands to feed the infants) and the mammals are developed from the reptilians (animals walking on earth surface with rubbing on it) as the evidences proved, in the tertiary period of the Cenozoic era. During the development of the human being perhaps the ultimate goal was the development of the brain.

Various myths about the origin and the development of human being are prevalent in the society. According to various olden religious books it is believed that various spiritual and divine powers have created all the living beings and it takes care for them. In this connection, according to our Hinduism; Lord Brahma has created the entire existence by his various organs, he has given birth to the human from his head, same as in the holy "Bible" God created the world in just six days and by the sixth day he created this human; Man came first and then the woman was created. Here about the holy BIBLE, it is clear that it has been written near about 2000 years back and we have known Lord JESUS just since then about 2 thousand or some more years. Here we know the history of our appearance just about then or some more about 3 or 4 thousand years back. But here a question stands that before Lord Jesus or any other history of man, there was the human on the territory and how they appeared? Was there a miracle for that? No, the only theory which gives the answer for the human appearance is EVOLUTION; Evolution of thousands and millions of years. So many imaginary theories are given from time to time but modern study on evidences has denied all these myths.

As we have known previously that human has come to this earth through a great duration of time and after crossing many more steps of the evolution. Human is a mammal (having breasts to feed milk to the infants) and has been converted from the other mammals named the old world monkeys. According to the Geological time scale the early man has developed during the tertiary period of the Cenozoic era about 13 million years ago.

It was just a co incident that human got appearance. It was the necessity of that time situations. Need of evolutionary characters of that time for the old world monkeys and the changes in the surrounding atmosphere were responsible for the appearance of the early man. The initiation of the fore limbs (legs) to be used as arms was the great reason for the evolution towards the ancestor species of early man, so the bipedal locomotion was adapted on spite of tetra pedal (walking on four legs). The process of evolution is so gradual that we can not notice in one or two generations but it takes thousands and millions of years and tens and hundreds of generations to be crossed with quite micro changes and many species have to sacrifice and have to lose their race then some of the species get existence with the law of "Survival of the fittest".

This process is so gradual that difference can't be seen in a general way, this process may be understood in example of the flowering of a plant, as we see a bud in any plant in the evening and next day morning a beautiful flower get split. It is not a miracle or magic but there is a process which produces a flower in a keen gradual but noticeable process. Same in the process of the evolution of human being the appearance of the movement on two legs was the great achievement. These changes were due to the necessity of that time circumstances and adopted the new characters for the basic needs of any living being "nutrition, protection and the reproduction". These old world monkeys started climbing on the trees for the first need of nourishment and started eating fruits etc on place of flash, for this they were unable to eat these fruits without help of any support. So the fore arms got adaptations through many generations and were called hands and these species started using the hands for both purposes as walking with four legs and holding something in hands same as today we see a monkey eating any edible thing such as fruits etc. The monkeys we see today are the branches of the species separated from the ancestor species millions of years back and some of the species got disappeared in the consequence of the struggle for the existence through the evolution. This bipedal locomotion was the basic foundation for the development of the BRAIN. When the two fore arms got started being used as hands on place of locomotion; they were being used as hands to do something other then walking and climbing on trees. These two hands were now free to do anything creative directed by the primitive brain. So for the emphatic utilization of these hands the brain got initiation towards development and evolution and the new revolution occurred when the brain was inspired towards creativity.

The brain was the greatest achievement for human that he has got today's top most position in the living world by the social status organized by the brain.

As far as we have known that about 450 million years ago the earth came into existence and then about 900 million years later, about 360 million years ago from today the first living being got appearance in form of a single cell. In the sequence, from simple to the complex, all the varieties of creatures got appearance through a gradual evolution in a huge period of 350 million years.

In this evolution man started taking place in the form of early man near about 13 million years ago. But the modern man of today with lots of inventions could become modern just 10000 years back.

The living creatures came into the existence in the simplest form and then developed up to the different varieties after crossing many more steps in a keen gradual process of millions of years and man is just a step among those steps but the latest one. Now, here we are going to discus the descent of man and the position among the Animal Kingdom of the living world.

MAN'S PLACE IN THE EVOLUTON

Man has been the great revolution in the evolution of the living world. Man has got the topmost position among all the creatures whatever plants animals or any other type of living beings. To understand the man's existence among the living creatures, we will have to go through the classification of all the living creatures. According to the Characters and the sequence of the evolution with the time man has classified in such a way as following:—

Biotic region of our earth is divided into 5 different KINGDOMS of the living beings according to the basic characters and developmental stages. These kingdoms are classified and distinguished with each other according to the origin of the species with the time, which species got the appearance first are in the initial kingdom of the classification:—

Kingdom MONERA:—The most primitive organisms and beginners of the living world Micro and first living organisms like viruses and bacteria. Various pathogenic Bacteria which are not visible by even microscopes but with the help of electronic microscopes we can see them, having the smallest size of the body. And the viruses are also known as the link between living and non living organisms because these are only active in any living organism or a culture media abundant with organic nutrients and do multiply in numbers within any living organism otherwise these show the activities like non living substances and could be kept till thousands of years without any changes and can be crystallized.

Kingdom PROTISTA:—The first True cells with all type of modern organelles'; e.g. unicellular organisms like Amoeba, Paramecium etc.

Kingdom FUNGI:—Multinucleated and also multi-cellular organisms like Fungus. These Funguses were the organisms which got the multi-cellularity first of all the living organisms during the evolution of the organisms.

Kingdom PLANTAE:—All type of photo synthetic and other varieties of plants.

Kingdom ANIMALIA:—All the living beings having sensory organs and nervous system and having locomotion, such as all the wild and domestic or aquatic animals cat, Rat, Monkey, Horse, Man etc.

Here man is the king of his Kingdom. According to characters and physical individuality man is classified by various standards as under:—

KINGDOM-ANIMALIA: Having all the Characters of an animal

PHYLLUM—Chordates: Having a spinal chord on its dorsal side for a well organized sense system of the body.

GROUP—VERTIBRATE: Vertebral column (small fragmental bones in pieces, 33 in numbers) in back bone for flexibility of the body and slightly s shaped for strengthening of the erect posture.

SUB PHYLLUM-GNATHOSTOMETA: Having jaws to chew eatables before ingestion for better digestion.

CLASS-Mammalian: Having Mammary (feeding capacity) gland for partial support to the infants and hairs on body to stabilize the temperature.

ORDER-PRIMATE: Having menstruation cycle for reproduction, grasping capacity; rounding the toe in all directions to hold things better.

FAMILY—HOMINIDAE: Bipedal locomotion and erect posture

Physically man by his characters is same as the other animals do, but he has got a great thing, the most developed brain having the biggest cerebrum (the main part of the brain located as front part of the brain responsible for all the mental activities). The emotions, mentality, thinking and memory all these functions are finalized by this part of the brain as so many researches have proved. And so on man has now developed a great social status by the development of cultural evolution. Man has got the intelligence, by which he can plan, express and tell any expression to each other by his voice and language. And by development his two fore arms into hands he can do whatever he wants or thinks.

By having bipedal (two feet) locomotion he started using his hands into some creative works and the next great achievement for the man was the brain which gave him the intelligence to handle the two hands in some great creations. These two hands were the greatest achievements for the revolution on the earth through the evolution of the living beings. In this way man's position in the evolution has been the topmost by overall views. Today man has got the rein of the world, he can develop or destroy the world, it depends upon him.

BASIC THEME FOR THE EVOLUTION OF MAN
(Evolutionary characters of man):—

There has been gradual evolution for creation of human being and during this evolution some special characters were developed according to the requirement as adaptations for the survival and these characters were transferred from generation to generations which were favorable. By the centralization of these characters evolution of man could have been possible. These evolutionary characters are going to be discussed as under:—

ERECT POSTURE—The only man is there in this entire world that has got this erect posture. This posture has been a great achievement for him. In this posture two feet are required for locomotion and the rest two becomes free by which he can use these in many more other works. These two hands have changed the map of the world. Man has held the world in his these two hands.

For this erect posture many more changes occurred during the evolution of man; here I would like to explain that these changes were the results of thousands of years through the mutations occurred in the generations and transferred by the genetic codes compiled in the DNA of the genes. This process is somewhat similar with the computer programming; where we put our requirement in the software as some specialized coding and the results we get what we need to finalize any type of programming. Any way we are to discuss the changes occurred in the human for this erect posture:—

    A. *Trunk portion became shorter and the legs became longer in compared with the other ancestor species.*

B. Bipedal locomotion (walking on two legs) developed and the rest two legs became hands and worked for some other works under supervision of brain.

C. The back bone became slightly "S" shaped for the strengthening of the body.

D. Skull (head) was modified for being straight on the vertebral column (back bone).

E. Jaws became shorter for less necessity of more power as the nutritional things were now selected on place of being raw; the face became straight.

BIPEDAL MOVEMENT—Monkeys, chimpanzees and apes etc. of this category walked on all four limbs so all limbs were called legs but man started by his two hind limbs so two limbs became legs and the rest two modified as hands. It was the process of millions of years through thousands of generations.

HOLDING CAPACITY (Grasping capacity)—Because of bipedal movement hands became free. The toe of the hand went to the opposite side of the other four fingers and so on the animal now could hold a particular thing easier and could be called the human being.

INTELLIGENCE—The most important evolution was the development of 'BRAIN' The brain was developed at the extent of the evolution, particularly CEREBRUM (the frontal part of the brain and most developed during the evolution of human; responsible for the cultural and creative activities)was the great achievement for this most advance animal of the nature. Along with the development of the brain; thinking, planning, emotions, expressions and languages were gradually developed.

SENSITIVETY—Man's sensitivity and excitement was developed towards the surrounding and the natural events. Both the eye were slipped towards front and concentrated towards one thing, this type of vision is called Binocular vision. Hearing capacity was developed but the external pinna of the ears went small. Smelling power became lesser and the snout pores concentrated downwards.

LESS HAIRS ON BODY—Gradual loss came to the body because of less necessity due to adopting the other shelters and coverings.

SKULL (Head)—Skull volume went bigger and from 400 cc, it went up to 1650cc to hold the much grown brain as the intelligence increased with the size of the brain.

FOOD—The olden ancestors of man were insectivorous, they became herbivorous according the circumstances changed with thousands and millions years spending by many generations, and then carnivorous (eating flash) with the time in lacking of favorable herbs and fruits etc. and so on they became omnivorous (both veg and non vegetarian).

EVOLUTION OF CULTURE—Only in man because of development of brain; the cultural activities appeared, so he became a social animal totally. This brain took about 13 million years to develop up to today's status and just 10000 thousand years back man could be totally modern and social.

BREEDING CAPACITY—Breeding rate became lesser with the development of the brain, as he could keep safe himself and the descendents. The menstrual cycle stated and because of social way his life became monogamy (one partner).

And so on these are a few characters which show that the man has evolved from his fore fathers and has reached up to today's cultured man because of the great thing "brain".

PROCEDURE—ORIGIN AND EVOLUTION OF MAN

The animal kingdom has a large variety of livestock and developed up to various directions, in the process of evolution and through this process the most advanced creature human has taken birth. Here again, I would like to explain that it has not been a miracle or a magic in a sudden way but it has been the result of millions of years worked on the natural world as the experiments occurred with time to time by the natural laws.

Here we are going to discuss the development of man. As we have known that man is not other than the animals living around us and also has been developed up to today's existence and he is the member of class "mammilla' (having mammary glands means feeding milk to the infants and having hairs on body for help to control the temperature inside the body) in the animal kingdom of the living world. All the basic characters of human are equalant to the group of some type of animals called primates such as bigger size of eyes and skull cavity (means much developed brain), females having menstruation cycle, less breeding capacity etc.

It was not a magic or a miracle occurred in a sudden way and time that the man got the appearance but it was the keen gradual process in which nature accused so many experiments from time to time with many of the generations of the living beings and in millions of years got the existence of human being. It was about 60 million years back when there was no man any where on the territory but the life was there in form of some olden living creatures and the primates were one of these species. The primates were developed from a rat type Shrews, which were the members of order insectivore means insect eating animals. These shrews were called elephant shrews because their snout and nose tip was long and also a long tail, their testes (the sperm generating organs in male) were inside the body, these were the insectivorous mammals with active small body, walking with jump on the earthen surface. These types of animals are even found today in the forests of African and some Asian regions. Just in these shrews the primary primate characters like human at the beginning stage were developed such as bigger size of eyes and skull cavity to hold the much developed brain, females having menstruation signs and not producing more than 1 to 3 infants at a time.

In this way; our olden ancestors were these Elephant shrews and just from these the other members of the order primates were developed. It was the time about 60 to 65 million years ago, when these ancestors started the evolution towards the primary members of primates. It was the time when the well known Dinosaurs were about to distinct and disappear and then the animals with small body started to develop and to spread over here and there on all the territory due to that time circumstances. And then the evolution of human took place in a gradual and sequent way from these primary small body primates in many steps and with a large number of species came and disappeared but some remained safe and continued their species survival and are still found in the living world but rest which could not continue their races and disappeared but remained as the evidences to tell their stories of their struggle of the existence in the form of fossils merged beneath the surface of Earth.

In this sequence, the appearance of human from these Elephant shrews took about 60 million years and thousands of species came and disappeared. First of all these shrews started aggression towards arboreal life about 60 million years ago, in the Paleocene Epoch of the Cenozoic era, these rat type small animals with pointed nose; called shrews as terrestrial ancestors, started semi arboreal life in the form of squirrel like long tailed shrews. These shrews had more characters like primates than the Elephant shrews such as snout organs were less developed, smelling capacity was lessen, bigger eyes onwards, testes developed, cones in eye retina were now created but feet were not adapted yet to climb up the trees, so they used to walk on the trees by their claws. They used to eat fruits exceptionally insects. In this way these Shrews were the primary primates and pre monkey ancestors of man. Some species of these are also found today in Malaya and India.

According the surrounding climate and abundance of the nourishments these shrews developed in three directions as the evidences and fossils found in various discoveries. From these shrews first of all some species adapted semi arboreal life as they started fruit eating along with being insectivorous and then some of these new species developed towards fully arboreal as they got the nutrition and security from their predators.

Another species was developed from these semi—arboreal shrews; called "Lemurs". These were arboreal and their hands and legs were adopted to hold the trees with their claws and their eyes were bigger. In some parts of Africa and Asia, some of these species are found even today.

And then one species appeared from these shrews, which became the ancestors of the preliminary man like animals such as apes etc.; named tarsiers. Tarsier's characters are fluctuating between pre monkey and pre man ancestor animals.

It was the time about 40 million years back, when from these semi-arboreal ancestors, the man like or man shaped ancestors were developed. In this connection with time, three directions of the descendent generations were appeared sequent. One way towards the generation of Monkey stock another towards Apes such as chimpanzee, gorilla, apes etc. and then some another species turned towards pre man ancestors which were the direct ancestors of human being.

Many fossils and evidences have been found which prove the gradual and sequent evolution of human being from the same ancestors in last millions of years and through thousands of generations with the mutations in the fundamental genetic network. So let's understand this development

Monkey stock:—About 40 million years ago two types of monkeys were developed from the pre-monkey primate ancestors. In which on one way "new world monkeys" were developed which had flat nose, snout outwards, long tail, 36 teeth and fingers clawed and the monkeys existing today are mostly descendents of those new world monkeys.

On other way "Old world monkeys" were developed which had the characters matching with somewhat human being such as narrow nose, snout pores nearer and downwards, tail some what small, nails on fingers, toe perpendicular to fingers and they had got the ability to transfer symbolical voice and were having 32 teeth. It means the new world monkeys adapted themselves to survive on the territory without more changes and were able to continue their generations in the same way as they were in the olden age but some species developed as the old world monkeys who had adopted themselves towards some another way and could not continue their generations in the same way but converted into some other species and the original species disappeared so they called the old world monkeys. In this way the pre ancestors of the man like animals as apes etc were developed from these old world monkeys which has been shown through the evidences discovered in recent times.

Ape stock:—Then in Miocene Epoch in the Geological time scale about 30 million years ago these old world monkeys evolved towards three directions first; small arboreal gibbon, yet found in deep forests in some of the continents, living on trees eating fruits and other vegetations. Secondly, heavy semi arboreal great Apes still found in deep jungles as we see in zoo, such as Gorilla and Chimpanzees etc. And thirdly "Hominid" man's ancestors started walking on claws on the territory and started to stand on feet.

Apes and human both are developed from the same ancestors so in these (specially Gorilla and Chimpanzee) and in man many equalities are seen which prove the evolution of both from the same ancestors such as; both having no tail, the Neck and Feet of both are longer than the similar species as monkeys etc, hands of both are able to hold a thing, legs adopted only for locomotion. Both are having larger volume of Brain and skull cavity and the memory centers are developed in both. Both have become omnivorous in spite of insectivorous. Both are capable to make symbolical voice, expression of smile, happiness sorrow, anger etc with facial muscles. Recent studies of DNA have also proven the similarity of human and apes, in which 98.5 % DNA of both is similar. Just 1.5% difference in the basic gene structure of DNA creates so great revolution in the human appearance. But it is also noticeable that this process of diversion and changes took how a long period of time about 25 to30 million years and some million generations with quite micro changes in each of the generation.

So many characters of both man and apes show the development of both from the some ancestors. Except these equalities there are many differences between man and apes; which show that these are related with different species but Along with being different species both are related with the same ancestors. There are many similarities between human and these apes such as absence of tail, longer neck and legs, hands able to hold things, legs adapted only for locomotion, along with this the volume of brain and skull cavity are larger and much centers of memory developed, both have become omnivorous from being insectivorous. The symbolical voice and efficiency of the expressions for smile happiness sorrow and anger etc has been

developed through the facial muscles has been developed in both the man and apes.

In this way these are some characters of both man and apes which show the evolution of both has been from any one or the same ancestors. In this sequence the ancestors and fore fathers of the Early man were developed from these apes like animals and some fossils found some time ago shows the links between the apes and human such as a fossil found in Africa named dryopithicus was having the linking characters between the apes and the early man as fore arms shorter, walking bent, and the volume of skull cavity was about 400 cc.

There has been a good successful and prospered life of early apes in India and Africa about 40 million years back, the period is named Miocene Epoch of the Cenozoic Era (according to the Geological time scale). At the End of this Epoch the big forests of some tropical region were destructed on a large scale due to some inverted weather conditions and were converted into big grass grounds. So that the apes were forced to live terrestrial life on spite of arboreal life along with this they started carnivorous life because of this deforestation, in the competition and lacking of herbs and trees as a great cause for them to be carnivorous. To get flesh they were helpless to run on the grass grounds; and so on for running they started bipedal locomotion along with straight posture. The most advance benefit by bipedal locomotion was to make two fore arms free as hands to do more works other than locomotion. In this way, this character was the cause for the development of the man from the early Apes. And so on the man-Pedigree separated from the apes with the erect posture and walking on two legs the new generations came into existence with the characters like human and called pre-man ape ancestors.

The development of modern man (Homo Sapience)in last 13 million years has been through four further steps—
1. Sub man
2. Ape man
3. Early true man or pre-historic man
4. True or modern man

All these forms are related with one species "Homo sapience". So these are least differing in physical but more different in cultural and mental activities. Here we are going to discuss these four developmental stages (The study of these stages of the development of man is mostly based on the fossils found by various scientists in the past.)

1. Sub man—In this step very old ancestors of man are developed from the pre man ape ancestors. Some particular fossils found in past which show the initiating characters of human existence differing from the early apes. Some fossils found in India at shivalik hills of Himalayas named Ramapithicus shows the characters as the human. These were 13 million years old and are called the first Hominid (human like). These had the characters like Incisors and canine teeth (front teeth), jaws and palate were like human and these used to walk more straight. These characters are oldest of the human pedigree.

2. Ape Man or near man-Further sub man developed to Ape man. On the character basis it is hard to say Ape or Man to these fossils found of this step generation. About 10 million to 4 million years old some fossils are found from Africa. A fossil named Australopithecus (means fluctuating characters between ape and man) Africanus was found by Mr. Raymond Dart, it was a skull of a baby of 5to 6 years of age in caves of Africa. The body of this early man was lighter (35 to 40 Kg in weight) and about 4 feet height and used to walk straight. Its skull cavity was 450 to 700 cc. It was omnivorous. Around some fossils some sticks, bones and accumulation of stones is found which shows they used these arms for security. The above characters show the gradual evolution from apes to man such as leaving arboreal life they started terrestrial bipedal movement and became omnivorous in lacking of required herbs. The brain was now much developed in comparison with the early apes and sub-man.

Another fossil found which was about 2-3 million years old named Australopithecus Robustus. Its weight was about 60 kg and these were more powerful than the Australopithecus Africanus and the jaws and teeth were longer as the herbivorous animals are having so perhaps these were also herbivorous. But these seem to be disappeared earlier may be due to lack of favorable herbs these were as a branch of human evolution.

Another fossil of Ape-man found in Africa named Australopithecus boisei. Mr Leaky in 1947 found a 1.75million year's old fossil. It was also named Australopithecus because it was having both the Ape and man like characters. Body of these used to be heavy about 70 kg the fingers of the fore arms were perpendicular with the toe like the hands, their nose was flatten, eye brows were now developed and their teeth and lower jaws were strong. As they were herbivorous so they could not develop during the evolutionary period and disappeared.

According to these fossil characters scientists believe that about 3 to 4 million years ago primary Ape man ancestors developed into two directions one way, heavier and on the other way the light weighted human like early man were developed. The heavier started arboreal and forest life with being herbivorous. But about 1 million years ago this branch was disappeared.

On the other way the lighter hominid (human like early man) started omnivorous and terrestrial life on open grounds. A complete fossil of an Ape-man (Australopithecus) type named "Lucy" about 1 million years old shows these characters very much clearly which opens the doors towards the early true man and tells that how the evolution of the earlier human went ahead.

3. Early True man Or pre historic man—About 1 million years ago a new type of early man developed from this Ape-man through this third step of the development of True man "homo Sapience" it was the beginning of the new species "homo".

Actually at the beginning of the bipedal locomotion the brain was not so developed and at that time the Australopithecus (Ape man) started using some things like stones bones etc. for hunting and security with the help of his hands. Then to control the use of his hands for more efficiency, the keen development of the brain initiated in a fluent way. Through this development many species came into existence and disappeared, it was the time of the history about 1.6 million years to 2hudred thousand years back, so these are called the pre-historic man and after crossing all these steps of early true man the most advanced species of human being has taken place.

During the 3rd step of Ape to man journey, the fossils found yet tells us about two types of species; first one has got the primary characters from the ape-man to early man. This pre historic human race originated about 1.6 million years ago. About 800 thousand years back in Africa this species used to live, their height was in between about 4 to 5 feet, weight was about 70 kg and cranial cavity's volume was about 680 cc and so on the brain was bigger than the Australopithecus(Ape man). This creature used to walk straight and used stone arms for safety and hunting.

Another fossil found of this early true man was called Homo erectus because adopting the erect posture for walking. About 600 hundred thousand years back this type of early man used to live. Their height was about 5 feet, weight was about 70 kg these were clearly straight walking but the eye brows were like the apes. These are called Java man because most of the fossils found in Java in Asia. Their cranial cavity was about 1000 cc and these were omnivorous, used fire and arms of stone and lived in java along with Africa and China. Another fossil found named Homo erectus Peckinansis near the caves of pecking in China. This type of early man's brain was more developed then the Java man and the volume of cranial cavity was about 1075 cc. They started using fire along with arms and lived in groups and were identified with time and place. Some evidences also clarify that these were cannibals also, their height was lesser but they used fire at a better scale. It means this early man was lived in deep jungles about 6 to 4 hundred thousand years back and the brain was initiated towards some advanced and new activities.

4.   TRUE OR MODERN MAN—As we see today the modern man in a common way that the human exists in it's this form as eternal but the evidences have proved the evolution of modern man after crossing thousands of species in last million years from the early man. So here we studied about the pre historic man Homo-erectus. It is defined by various scientists that the modern man (homo Sapience) has taken birth just from these Homo erectus. According to the evidences it happened in various times and on the different territory on the earth independently. There are various sub species in the Homo Sapience generations because of more equalities but slight differences.

Various fossils are found in rocks of this species which show the appearance about 2to 3 hundred thousand years ago. Two sub species of this class are very important here during the evolution of *human being. One species named Neanderthal man lived in Europe near about 150 thousand years ago and disappeared about 35000 years back. These were about 1.6 meters in height their eye brows and nose were broader and the cranial cavity was near to the modern man about 1450 cc. These were the creatures that may now be called the people. They used to create beautiful arms and also capable to hunt Rhino and Elephant. These were now become social and the division of labor was invented till then. They believed religion and existence of soul, buried death bodies according their traditions. They were also the cannibals started using the leather of animals to cover their bodies. No cultivation and animal husbandry was done but arrows, blades knives like arms were now prepared and used for hunting. These can be called the direct ancestors of the modern man but could not be called the modern man itself because of less development of mind. These were able to talk some usual sentences because of the development of the voice. This early man lived in Europe Asia and also in Africa.*

Another species named Cro-Magnon was lived in the deep forests of Europe near about 35 to 40 thousand years back. These were the descendents generations of the Neanderthal man. This species is called Cro-Magnon because the fossils of these were found in Cro-Magnon caves of France. Both the Neanderthal and Cro-Magnon species also lived along with but the Cro-Magnons were more advance in intelligence so they dominated the Neanderthals and captured the power on the territory. So this Cro-Magnon man is called the past's modern man due to advance mental appearance and also scientifically named same as the modern man; HOMO SAPIENCE-FOSSILIS. The Cro-Magnon man were about 6 feet in height skull was same as the modern man face broader eye brows were sharper and thin same as the modern human being and the cranial cavities volume was about 1600cc nearer to modern man. These used to live in caves, in small families, used food after cooking were also artistic and created art on the rocks of the caves. They used edge and arrows with bow made with elephant teeth. But agriculture and animal husbandry could not be discovered by them. Although these were more intelligent then the Neanderthals but they kept marriage relations with them. These were the direct ancestors of the modern man and about 10000 years back these were disappeared and the new modern man with the great intellectual property "intelligence" appeared.

The modern man of today is totally same as the Cro-Magnon man was but only cultural development has created the difference between these two verities of man. About 10000 years ago this man developed in Eastern Asia near Caspian Sea. This is the most modern man among all the early generations of its kind and also the most advance and intelligent man as a living being. Straight posture, bipedal locomotion, complexity of brain, longer legs then the fore-arms, beautiful face, broad forehead etc. are the physical properties of it. Cast, religion, social network, agriculture are some properties which show the progressive man towards modernization. After crossing certain period of time modern man has got birth from the Cro-Magnon man. The cultural development has been the reason for the evolution for this process. Agriculture, animal husbandry, development of languages and other communication ways, use of arms, forming small families are the cultural activities developed with time to time.

So the period from Cro-Magnons to modern man took about 10thousands years. The Cro-Magnon man lived as the early man in the deep jungle in the same form as the other animals do but with initiation of some advanced and creative activities towards convenience for the living and spent about 30 thousand years period ;then the new generations of these Cro-Magnons started utilizing their brain to fulfill their required activities for living. This period of the cultural development of the modern man of last 10 thousand years is called the STONE AGE; when the early man started using stones for hunting and safety. This Stone Age is divided in three parts of period.

1. Initial Stone Age—The man of this period was the pre and beginner of creative and mental activities and some primary cultural activities were initiated. Man had started using bones and stone arms for hunting. But no agriculture or animal husbandry could be done by them. This period was spent by man about 10 to 12 thousand years back and till 7 to 8 thousand years back it is called the initiating stone age(Paleolithic period) of about 2-5 thousand years.

2. Middle stone age—This was the time when the historic man started understanding nature and natural phenomena and started some primary systems of agriculture, also started to tame the animals and got the ways to utilize the animal husbandry for their convenience. Now in this period they learnt some usual sentences of language and

started some primary system of reading and writing. The necessity of counting numbers was now required and the primary numeric system was discovered in this period which was about 6-7 thousand years back from today and called the Mesolithic period of the modern man's journey of the existence with the progressive intelligence.

3. New and latest period of STONE AGE—In this period man could learn Agriculture at a better scale and started family life in small huts and social life initiated for the convenience of each other. This was the period when the clothing invented which was of leather at the beginning but became cloths later; also the use of utensils could be learnt in this period. It was about 5 thousand years back from today.

Then after this Neolithic—period (new stone age) we know much about the history of man through our literature found in various books and ethics and also the mythological literal material written or created in last 3-4 thousand years and also through many evidences, fossils and discoveries in last few years. **Then after this stone age, about 3 thousand years from today a metal bronze was invented which was very much useful for the daily requirement such as for water and for food to be served or stored etc. This era is called the Bronze Age went up to 2000 years. And then about 1200 BC ago the metal Iron was invented and the new era named Iron age initiated which brought revolution in the activities of human being. Then the great revolution came in the field of cultivation by the invention of equipments like sickle, spade, axe etc which helped man to create more productive land for agriculture and the forest lands converted into the lands for agriculture; so that the problem of food was now solved and man started making small huts near the natural water sources such as rivers lake ponds etc. and began to do cultivation. In this way the need of that time became the convenience later and small groups of families became villages later, the division of labor was now done at a better scale. Then about 3 thousand years from today in 600 BC the literal language was invented and the primary ways of writing were initiated and the oldest literature we have found is from this period.**

So on, we know much about the history of human pedigree through different literature. In this way this was the story through

which man came to the existence and how it became the king of this beautiful world. Now man has become so creative and enthusiastic about the nature. Nature has given us more and more beautiful things but man just changes the design of these things for his convenience through getting the two hands free and the brain inside his head to control the overall activities of these two hands for many creative and productive works. And now man is trying to get up and also to reach the moon and some planets like mars and trying to find life or the possibilities of life there.

6

Diversity in Life

(Uncountable number of living creatures)

Today *we see a drastic variety of living creatures and organisms everywhere on the territory and also in the water. Even in the air there are millions of living tiny organisms found. Were all these present here since the birth of the EARTH? NO, even human has got the history of just about some million years old and which has been in various species with less developed brain conquered the typical circumstances with time to time. Similarly all the creatures existing on or round the GLOBE have*

not appeared as a magic or miracle but have been the result of the natures' experiments done for their survival from time to time. In this connection, the first Living-Being has got birth about 3600 million years ago in the form of unicellular organism. And then that micro organism started developing into various forms according to environmental conditions, before that there was no life on the earth for about 900million years, which is called the AZOIC ERA means the era without any signs of life. And then the life began to grow in the water in form of unicellular organism with some basic activities of life like ingesting nutrients, growing and dividing into two new living organisms and the life split towards increasing in numbers and the revolution began on the noble earth. Crossing many more steps millions of species have been split. In this journey a lot of species came to the existence and disappeared because of unfavorable environmental conditions. After all this there a drastic variety of living beings is remained today, it will be millions in numbers. it is believed that the number of extinct species might have been 50 to 100 times that of the existing living beings today.

Today's living world has been prospered in a way from simple to the complex creatures. First of all the link between living and non-living beings the VIRUSES converted into a living being in form of unicellular organisms called BACTERIA. And from this micro-organism bacteria various organisms, living beings like Algae, fungi, plants and animals etc, are developed in a gradual and sequent way according to continuously changing atmosphere and environmental conditions and with time to time. One type of organism changed into various other varieties along with these conditions and also due to different climatic places on the territory. The signs which have clarified that the first living creature began in the deep oceanic aqua in form of micro organization with primary signs of life; named virtually the "pre life constitutions".

Darwin a great philosopher has described that a living being which is capable of fighting with the inverted environment and those species that get victory are free to survive successfully. So what varieties we see today are able to bear present conditions, rest of these which could not bear these conditions, disappeared. It means which could adapt themselves according to the circumstances got the continuity of life onwards with some new characters. In this consequence of adaptations the accumulations of new characters in forthcoming generations creates a quite new species from the original one and in this way the new species are taking place to conquer the survival in the changing atmosphere as habitat and weather etc. Many more experiments are being done on various varieties of today in form of various environmental events as different natural phenomenon in the climate and as a result of these experiments some new descendent generations are produced from the original ones but which are capable to survive in the new environment are supported by the nature to live and continue their generations in these new forms; rest descendents disappears which are not capable to survive in that time environment. In this way, nature produces a large quantity and variety of the descendent living beings, so that some of these could survive and rest die. This is why that multiple times of the living species have been disappeared. Ultra violet rays coming from the Sun, different temperature zones of the earth, changing of seasons time to time, the uneven geography of earth, conversions of day and night, have made the chances for the adaptations to conquer the survival on the territory for any living being. These conditions make chances for "Mutations" in the genetic consequences of any living being which is finally responsible for a new activity and physical appearance of any living creature.

Here the fundamental point or reason for the variation in generations and different species is the Recombination of the genetic matter of the male and female gametes during the fertilization of an egg. The variation changes a generation to another and so on different Flora and Fauna are found here as a result.

Since the origin of life, the adaptations have given birth to the variations and diversity. So Diversity and adaptations are the basis for the Bio-Evolution in which the new species get success in the struggle for the survival and becomes a new species; a living being quite different from the original one who conquers the inverted circumstances of nature. As the conditions became the living beings adapted themselves for the survival and accepted new activities and physical abilities for food and other vital necessities but those living beings could not survive who did not accept new adaptations and new characters for the new circumstances. Mutation played a great roll in creating diversity by changing the basic gene structure. In this long journey many species came and extinct during these conflictions.

An example of this genetic mutation is also me and my family, as we are the carriers of Thalassemia a type of blood disorder in which Hemoglobin is unstable and the affected requires blood from donors; a gene responsible for the formation of red blood cell in human being is linked with the 11th pair of the chromosomes of the DNA strand, where a systematic and sequent form of nitrogenous basis is built with in it which synthesizes some particular types of protein structure of the hemoglobin of the RBC. If a little bit changes in the consequence occurs it results the formation of hemoglobin with a fault and the victim requires blood to be given from outside. The DNA is having a coding of 4 nitrogenous bases A, G, C, T (adenine, guanine, cytosine and thiamin). The repetition in various modes of these bases results into a type of protein synthesis and any character of the living being. In this consequence I am the carrier of the DNA with a changed sequence of the nitrogenous bases where G (Guanine) base is added to the normal sequence additionally and becomes abnormal genetic status of the DNA. As a result of this the person affected with this fault becomes the carrier of the Thalassemia gene where the size of RBC becomes less in which the MCV (Mean Corpuscular or cell Volume) goes below 70 fl (fl: a unit of the tiny measurement). Which show the smaller size of the cell? As far as we know, this abnormal genetic status results as favorable to the person in his own life by saving him from the endemic disease Malaria through making the small size of the RBC and escaping from the attack of the parasite plasmodium causing Malaria. In this way the carriers of the thalassemia are most probably safe from the malaria. So the mutation in the genetic status of the DNA responsible for the formation of Hemoglobin in the red blood cells helps the human from the disease malaria. But as an adverse effect of this change in the consequence of the DNA becomes dangerous and lethal if two carrier of this changed DNA marries and produces the next generation with this defaulted DNA results the disease of Thallassemia major in probability of 25 % in the forthcoming children. In this way the children taken birth with the carrier or with normal genetic status survive but the child who carries both the thalassamea gene could not survive due to the defaulted RBC with unstable Hemoglobin. These tiny changes in the genetic DNA as the mutations gives new characters to the race to conquer the adverse circumstances of the surroundings are not always favorable but some times these changes becomes lethal. So for the existence in the new atmosphere it is necessary to have some changed characters and adaptations to conquer the struggle of living world.

As the theories say that the preliminary conditions of earth became responsible for the generation of life during a certain period. The preliminary gases such as carbon mono-oxide(CO), carbon dioxide(CO2), Nitrogen(N2), Hydrogen(H2)and water in vapor form converted into some complex substances like, Ammonia (NH3), Methane(CH4), Hydrogen cyanide (HCN), etc. according to that time situations. And then from these substances, volcanoes, uv-rays, lightening, etc. energy sources given a chance to create Organic substances which are responsible for life as Amino acids, sugars, Nitrogenous bases etc. From these micro molecules life can't be originated but polymers of these micro molecules like protein and nucleic acids are the direct constitutional source of life. By repeated evaporation the concentration of micro molecules would have increased, so those got the minimum energy for polymerization. In this way the circumstances given place to the pre life conditions on the Earth during millions of year's period. The primary organization like a cell having these micro molecules started taking other matters from surroundings through adsorption. In this way internal molecules arranged in such a way that the molecules were adsorbed selectively. So these constitutions of protein structures became protienoid micro spheres and were called pre life constitutions and became the first living Cell. It is observed that when a hot mixture of polypeptides (small constituting units of protein) is cooled up to some special circumstances then protienoid micro spheres are created, which show some activities like living beings. In fact these were the micro spheres which developed up to various species according with time and circumstances occurred.

Along with the origin of life some necessary changes came to happen to it. Adaptation according to the changes in he surrounding atmosphere is one of the preliminary characters of the life; which has become fundament for the variations. And as a conclusion of these variations a great field of diversity is obtained; which is quite necessary for evolution and survival of a living species. Diversity is necessary for evolution and each creature has got a capacity for evolution. In this consequence life started in the form of a living cell as the simplest form has now developed up to drastic range of various micro organisms like Bacteria and fungi etc, plants and animals in millions of numbers of today. From the origin of life to the present existence many more creatures as millions of species came to exist and disappeared in the challenging atmosphere of the planet, which could adapt themselves remained existing, rest disappeared.

After all, by whichever method, the living being come to the existence was dependent on the surrounding nutritional elements for nutrition. The living beings came initially were not auto synthetic so they got nutrients from surrounding for energy. And so on with the time these would have exhausted in the surrounding due to less chemosynthesis process in proportion with the nutritional rate of the living beings. So only those creatures got existing which could get nutrients, rest disappeared. Natural selection would also have accepted those mutations which could help the creatures to get nutrients. In the beginning creatures used prepared nutritional elements till those were in abundance. But later in the lack of those, other elements would have used which were not in their originated form but in a converted form. So nature would have selected those creatures which could adapt this option of nutrition. As in a way, a substance is available in surrounding but later on it is being exhausted, in such a condition any cells or creatures which have got a mutant gene which can induce to create this substance from some other substances available in the surrounding then these cells or creature could survive in this condition.

In this way the simplicity converted into complexity. For the requirement of basic nutrition, chain type mechanism was generated through the mutations and adaptations. For example, a substance A is needed to any living cell, was available and was being generated by Chemo-synthesis process of the nature but later on it is being exhausted then a living cell which has got an enzyme 'a' which can create this substance A from another available substance B, then this living cell could survive; and so on if this substance B is also exhausted so there will be again necessity of another mutant gene which could produce the basic nutritional substance from some other substances of the surrounding. In this way a chain type mechanism gave birth to the variations and new bio chemical reactions developed in the preliminary cells. Many more creations like these preliminary cells would have been generated in the oceanic water. Some of these would have been destroyed but some of these remained by having favorable conditions and would have grown up in size. Because of grow in size, after a certain period, these creatures divided into pieces and each piece showed characters same like its generating cell. Possibly this would have been the primary system of cyto-genesis and re-production.

According to the surrounding's nutrition, the living creature started struggling in life. At beginning the mode of nutrition was adsorption as a simple way of ingestion from the surrounding to get energy to finalize their vital activities. When the first living being came there was a great prosperity of nutrients but gradually as the consumption increased, nutrients went exhausted with the time of some thousand years and the competition began among those simple creatures of the same species. FERMENTATION (in which a glucose molecule is converted into ethanol and produces carbon dioxide; so this resulted into a lot of energy for vital activities for a living being) was the mode to get energy from organic substances as the first source of energy; which de-gradated the organic substances available at that time. So on a new way of the struggle initiated to get nutrients from surrounding living bodies and Heterotrophic mode of nutrition got encouragement, another way of competition among that time living beings was to be faced as inter-species competition for nutrition, arose. In lack of nutrients, this competition among those time living creatures for nutrition initiated heterotrophic mode of nutrition and the heterotrophic creatures developed a drastic range and variety for nutrition and number of primary micro-organisms. But in such a condition a situation occurred in which it was difficult to carry on life onwards. Activities of living beings resulted, some changes in the climate. Fermentation (the first system for getting energy in living beings) enforced carbon-di-oxide in the surroundings and finished the organic substances which were essential for life, though which were available in abundance yet now went exhausted within some million years. Then another system of nutrition took place;' Photo-Synthesis'. It was an autotrophic system of nutrition, in which carbon-di-oxide was used as raw material in presence of solar energy and organic substances are formed with bigger molecules. This autotrophic system filled up the lacking of organic nutrients. As the evidences have shown that this process of auto tropism was initiated in preliminary form in an algae; found flouting on oceanic surface in some particular regions named

'Blue Green Algae'. The process of Photosynthesis in its preliminary form started utilizing carbon di oxide and liberated Oxygen. Then this free Oxygen made a revolution in the environment of living world by oxidizing all the substances and elements available on the territory. Atmosphere became oxidizing and most of the elements were oxidized (such as Hematite, Alumina [Al2O3] etc.). This was the period when the Ozone (O3) gas would have created because of more oxygen and with the help of sharp Ultra-Violet rays. This ozone gas condensed in the atmosphere at higher level of the particular region of the environment. This ozone layer protective to all the living creatures from the harmful ultra-violet rays coming from Sun. As the formation of this Ozone layer occurred the chances for chemical reactions decreased and the Evolution got another way for biological evolution in still produced creatures. And then the new mode of getting energy from the organic substances available in surrounding and produced through auto synthesis by the process of photo-synthesis. So when this process of producing organic substances from carbon di oxide with the help of sunlight a new way of nutrition appeared and through this process much more oxygen was released and this oxygen gave more energy from the organic substances during respiration through oxidizing (burning) those organic molecules rather than the old system of fermentation. Both the Auto tropes and heterotopous living beings started this new but more capable AEROBIC respiration, where oxygen was consumed and carbon di oxide was liberated. This availability of sufficient oxygen opened the ways for Bio-Evolution at a large extent. Life got variations through thousands of generations according to the requirement, at the beginning, in connection with the surrounding atmosphere; as weather, preys, nutrition etc. Adapting variations is one of the infra-structural characters of life to conquer the new and invert circumstances of the nature. Each creature adapted new characters with the time and carried forward their generations. These changes occurred in beginning, became the cause for the diversity in life. Every creature has got the efficiency for evolution to overcome the new atmosphere of the nature. So smallest form of life has now developed up to millions of verities of living creatures as micro-bacteria, plants and animals. From the origin of life to today's scenario of life millions of creatures got the existence but which could adapt themselves with the changing situations of the atmosphere, got the survival in the changed form.

First of all the non living substances were there on the earth. Then the viruses with only a protein covering around a DNA or RNA molecule, got birth, as the primitive molecule of DNA got invented in the nature. These viruses were the link between living and non living substances because these show some characters of both the living and non living substances such as these viruses can be crystallized for thousands years like the non living and again when they get the favorable conditions as availability of nutrients; organic material as glucose etc or entered in any living being cell, start multiplying like living being and reproduces again. So these viruses initiated the living beings and the first life got split. The living beings have developed from simple to complex forms in accordance with time since about 3.5 billion years to today through a systematic and sequent keen gradual evolution. In this period a drastic range of living creatures have been developed and prospered on the earth. In this struggle millions of species came and disappeared may be 50 to 100 times than the existing living creatures in the world. It is so because the creatures who could adapt the new characters in the inverted climate got the existence and survived further and these new characters were carried forward in their forthcoming generations to make the descendent generations capable to overcome the difficult circumstances and so they got some new defensive factors. Then with the accumulation of more new characters crossing some generations a quite new creature is born to be called a new species strongly different from the original one. Here it is to be noticed that this new species shows a great difference from the olden species but basic and fundamental criteria is same in the basic and structural individuality. For example we usually talk that our forefathers were monkeys but generally it is known that a long ago our generations of forefathers were developed from Apes. Recent studies have discovered the difference between Apes and Man that just 1.5 % of DNA is changed during the evolution of man and this process took 13 million years. We can imagine how a long period requires the process of evolution to create a new species. This difference of 1.5% in the DNA is the basic reason for the evolution of human because the physical appearance of any creature is finalized just through the DNA. This keen gradual differentiation in the DNA resulted, new characters and the physical appearance such as development of the cerebral cortex in the brain, straight posture of the body, loss of hairs, longer legs and shorter hands with more grasping capacity through perpendicular toes to hold things better etc. But the basic living activities are same between them such as for getting energy both need nutrition and respiration for oxidizing it in which both take oxygen as intake and carbon di oxide as out-put, both are giving birth to their infants and feed them with mothers milk, the process of growing and aging is same there, both are having menstruation in females as a process of ovulation for fertilization of the egg and to reproduce their descendents to carry forward the species with their individuality. Thousands of generations would have crossed millions of years with some slight changes from time to time in the generations of the apes would have resulted the modern human being with his own individuality. So all the living beings are similar at the basic structural and activities level but some slight changes with the time perhaps years in thousands and millions have resulted the variations and diversity of the living world.

The living beings are classified and distinguished by the scientists in five Kingdoms according to their developmental stages and other characters. The co existence of these living beings has created a special Ecosystem on the earth:—

1   Kingdom MONERA:—Most olden creatures having prokaryotic (simple and olden cell structure) cells including bacteria, blue green algae etc.
2   Kingdom PROTISTA:—Eukaryotic (true and modern cell organelles) these were also single cell creatures but with much developed cells with more organelles such as mitochondria including Algae and Fungi etc. These were much developed than the Monera kingdom creatures.
3   Kingdom PLANTAE:—Photosynthetic multi cellular organisms, including all the plants and herbs.
4   Kingdom fungi:—Pathogenic multi cellular organisms
5   Kingdom ANIMALEA:—There are more than 1 million species yet known of the animals which are developed step by step and from time to time.

There are millions of species for each Kingdom and all these have developed according to their surrounding conditions and climatic situations. Nutrition and mode of nutrition has been the basic object for all this evolutionary process. Situations after situations affected *the body shape and the activities of the creatures and the life got the great diversity full of enthusiasm and wonders of varieties.*

When nature got a great success by developing the molecule of first DNA (Deoxyribonucleic acid) ; informatics and multiplying element of the cell and unit of life, the life began here because the DNA could replicate and make copies of itself and also could create a protein structure by transcription which is an essential part of a living body. From that time till today life has tried to get better and in this connection the changes and diversity with the atmospheric changes has taken place. And so on, beneath the oceans to the infinite sky nature has tried its best in search of the best and man is the result of this continuous variation in the living world concluding towards the diversity. The variety of living creatures we see today as different types of animals, different types of plants with a huge amount of flora and there are millions of the species invisible to us but existing surround us are the result of the genetic recombination with millions of years period. Each of the living phenomenon whether a plant, an animal or any micro-organism existing on the planet is quite unique and is only of it's own kind, as any of the moment of time could not be repeated any of the second, minute or a particular time could not be repeated again. So the living creatures seems to be of same species but may not be quite similar at all because there will be some or a little difference in the genes of the DNA which would result the creature of its own kind. We see millions of people in the world all are same as human beings with the same basic characters such as getting nutrition, living in the same manner for their routine, giving birth to an infant, growing as a child, even the physical appearance is same as two eyes, two ears, two hands and two legs, single a tongue and nose; means a basic structure and activities are quite similar and we can say each of the person as a human being and generally it is called a mankind. Here we see all the persons are called individuals as a unit and all are same in a common or general aspect but actually each of the individual is different from the other one and is of its own kind because as, a moment can not be reversed or repeated; same as it an individual even a creature is not repeated in any manner at all because a particular creature is born after the recombination of the genetic matter of *its ancestor male and female forefathers and at each of the time of recombination of the genetic matter the sequencing of DNA is changed weather in a small or a large bases. The basic gene structure is same during all the recombination but some micro differences occur in each of the birth of the descendent; which sometimes becomes favorable as developing of new characters and adaptations to fight and overcome the inverted climate and conquer the survival in future and take the generations in future. But sometimes these changes in genes become lethal for the forthcoming newborns because of developing any type of defect in the DNA resulting defect in the structure or activities. So the changes in the gene structure of any living being occurred to overcome the inverted situations of the nature and to survive successfully in future. Through this recombination of the genetic matter nature gives more chances to the next generations to get victory in the new climate to live successfully and fulfill their living activities as nutrition, protection and reproduction for the survival, but rest, which couldn't adapt and died with the time.*

In this way, we see a drastic variety of living creatures around us, are not appeared by any miracle or a magic in a sudden way or in a sudden moment. But each of the creatures has been developed through a keen gradual process; called the Evolution and the species of different creatures are the result of the adaptations and mutations acquired in millions of years for the existence and to conquer the conflictions of the natural events surrounded in the atmosphere of the Blue Heaven called the GLOBE.

7

Aim of Life

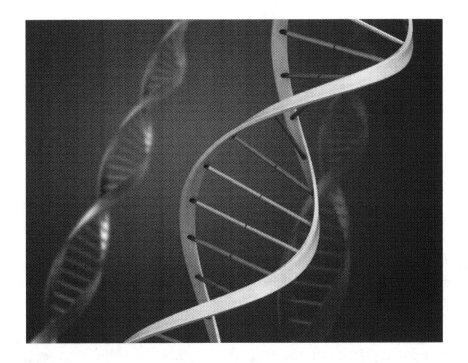

*H*ere "Aim of life" means not only the aim of any human's life but the aim of being a living being. Here the question arises of the intention of any living being or creature that for what purpose any living phenomenon lives and acts in its life? We see millions of creatures surround us; all are active and living in their own way finalizing its many living activities. But now we have to know why they are doing so? We see many animals' birds' small creatures' even micro organisms; even invisible to us but we know that they are surround us and different types of plants are also alive and are also living in their own manner. What is the Aim of their living?

Actually all this drama or system is for the FLOW OF ENERGY. We know that any work or function is finalized only through the energy and any living activity also requires the energy to finalize the vital activities and all the creatures and living organisms act initially to get energy through various nutrients. As we have discussed that any living creature requires three fundamental needs to be defined as a living being; Nutrition, protection and reproduction. In this consequence each living being takes nutrition from the surrounding atmosphere, finalizes its vital activities such as growing, protecting itself from the other species surround it, and also for reproduction to continue the race further. So any living being we see around us acts just towards these three basic needs and struggles for the survival and the existence of the race.

So to understand the Aim of being a living being we will have to go back millions of years with the life's origin and the evolution through which thousands of modes of nutrition, protection and reproduction got their ways with the time through the evolution of this period of three and a half billion years struggle of the living species of millions in number adapting different climates of the tremendous Earth. As we have known that the life has got today's enormous form after crossing millions of years and after a long term periods and many steps of different millstones of millions of generations of the living beings. The sequence of this existence of the living phenomena has been from 'simple to the complex'. It has been already concluded that before the life, about 3.6 billion years ago, all the simplest elements like hydrogen, nitrogen, carbon etc. started reacting and created the complex substances according to that time situations (proven by Nobel prize winner scientists Miller and Urey by creating that time the circumstances of the Earth; produced different types of carbohydrates and proteins from these simple elements in the laboratory). As it is clear that the climate of Earth was too hot more than hundreds of degrees of the temperature, as we see volcanoes beneath the crust of the Earth having too hot temperature with hundreds and thousands of degrees which show how the earth was in those times before the origin of the life here, even water and many other substances were in gaseous form, but as the temperature went cooler the steam converted into water and rained multiple times so the oceanic water was produced and the surface of the earth became cool with the time. This process of cooling in the atmosphere of the globe took about 900 million years and then the first living creature split on earth in form of unicellular organization with micro molecules of proteins and nucleic acids.

So those time situation on earth generated complex substances like ammonia, methane, ethane etc.; and these complex substances started reacting and created complex compounds like molecules of Glucose(carbohydrates), amino acids, fatty acids etc. (essential substances for any living structure). These newly formed organic substances concentrated in the oceans and when these macromolecules got the minimum energy for polymerization and some enzymes for the stimulation of the chemical reactions and these reactions produced the essential macro molecules for life like protein (polypeptides) and Nucleic Acids. As this concentrated fluid of the sugars and amino acids got energy through various sources like volcanoes, solar rays, ultra-violet rays etc. started condensing and polymerization and produced life making sub stances in following sequences:—

Sugars + sugars = polysaccharides (carbohydrates)
Fatty acids + glycerin = Lipids
Amino Acids + Amino acids = Proteins
Nitrogenous Bases + sugars = phosphates = nucleotide
Polymers of Nucleotides = nucleic acids

In this way the macromolecules like carbohydrates, fats, proteins and nucleic acids were produced in the deep oceans in those time; this process of production of these macromolecules is not continue in that way in any place on the Earth because those circumstances are not found today but the production process for those macromolecules is being done by various types of plants with the help of Photosynthesis and becomes the basic part of nutrition in an Ecosystem.

As the macromolecules got favorable conditions, necessary pH, having ion structure, converted into special complex units as droplets which were surrounded by water molecules. So just in the water some water molecules with the concentration of the macromolecules changed into some special units. Slowly these units would have adsorbed other compound molecules from the surrounding water. And then a certain time these units would have created a membrane by an special arrangement being selective for the input and the output of the molecules. (An experiment showing creation of life-when a mixture of polypeptide [protein's small units] molecules is heated at some specific temperature then protein micro spheres are created and these show some characters like living cell. Then, when these micro units got the multiplying capacity by having nucleic acids it got the honor of being a living being.

In this way, it was just a co incidence that the life began here. So those water molecules having macromolecules became the living cell with 'the aim of' "transportation" of various molecules from outside the cell to inside and vise-verse. And when the specific molecules arranged around this creation, it started a selective membrane with the choice of selected molecules ingesting and excreting. Those creations selected those molecules which were essential for their growth and multiplication. These organizations of specific molecules started reproducing through multiplication increased in numbers; even millions crossed thousands and millions of years. These multiplied and grown until the organic substances essential for their growth and multiplicity exhausted. And as the consumption increased the essential organic material went about to exhaust. So these creations now required some other mode for creation of these essential substances from some other available substances and some new types of living beings got birth. So this initiation in the mode of nutrition became the reason for the huge amount of variations in the world.

Here life has been just a co incidence on the Earth and when the first living being got existed, its first want was to get nutritional substances from the surroundings. And the second want was to maintain and keep living itself. The third one was that to keep continue the existence through the race. *In this way the physical mode of aim of life may be defined in three points:*

1   *To get nutrition*
2   *Protection:—To keep maintained and save the body (struggle)*
3   *To reproduce same units for the existence of the race and to get more efficiency in the struggle for the survival*

1 To get nutrition:—

As we have known that the dramatic network of the living world is through the flow of energy and all the living creatures act just to get energy to finalize its living and vital activities. This energy can be obtained from any nutritional substance available around the living beings.

Nutrition is the first requirement of any creature; whatever it is an animal or a unicellular organism like bacteria or it may also be a cell of a plant. The life got birth in the form of an organization in the oceanic water with abundance of nutritional organic substances of that time circumstances of the Earth. This organization was made of just some specified constituents molecules, in which some molecules arranged around and created a selectively permeable body like a membrane, started getting in and out the selected molecules. Now these bodies required some energy and constituents to keep maintained and grow up it. So it started selecting molecules beneficial to itself from the surrounding.

The concept of nutrition is connected with birth of life because the term 'living means to get nutrition and utilize it and get energy to grow up keep maintained the existence of the body and race.

To have existence as a living being the nutrition is a most necessary requirement for a living being. When the life began the creatures started in the smallest form as an organization which started ingesting macro molecules such as carbohydrates, amino acids etc essential for the energy and structure.

As these living bodies got reproduction and started multiplying in numbers the necessity of nutrients increased and a time came when the nutrients went exhausted Along with the changing favors of the atmosphere and in lack of so required nutrients and due to reaching in different areas of the climate of the earth the creatures required new modes and new matter for nutrition for getting energy to grow up and utilize it for it's vital activities. So on these smallest living bodies started getting new forms and adaptations to achieve nutrition with the help of mutations through sudden changes in the genes (Genes are those formulations which used to have the themes of any activity or any structure of the living body). In this way these smallest living bodies gave birth to different types of micro organisms

with time as the habitat and habits changed to get nutrients and to overcome the circumstances of the nature and gave initiation to the world of enthusiasm and wonders of diversity.

We can understand the adaptations and diversity through some examples as further. We know that in our social existence there have been hundreds and thousands of inventions with the time to facilitate our living; in this connection it is clear that how large variety has been diversified from the initiation of an invention at its primary and simplest form such as man invented fire about 10 to 20 thousand years back, what was its form and use at that time only to fire in the dark and the fire was kept burning because those people did not know how to generate a fire again. It was just a co incidence that they understood the use of fire and the invention. Later on the uses of fire increased with the time as man started cooking food and burning lamps, burning lamps to keep the dangerous animals away, but as the time changed man understood the multiple uses of fire and now we know how useful the fire is in the human's life as different types of industries use fire at their basic system such as furnaces, melting units even cutting of heavy metals etc is done with help of fire ; In this way the invention of fire was a co incidence and used at a limited manner initially but now after a long period the use of fire has been diversified in multiple ways. Same the initial smallest creatures used the primary mode of nutrition and adapted new ways and modes with the time. Here all types of uses of fire are in continue and the olden mode are also used even today; it means all types of modes are in continue and used in any of the manner and all the types invented with the time are used with its diversity same the living beings invented by nature with time to time are continue with their individuality and specialty as new species with different modes of nutrition, protection and reproduction through millions of years.

Another example can help to understand the diversity and adaptations; we know that the invention of wheel has been a long ago about 20 to 30 thousand years back, exact belonging of time and place is not clear but it is clear that the invention of wheel has created a revolution in the field of transportation and the industrial equipments. Initially man used the wheel as an equipment to transfer heavy things from one place to another as making different types of carts and sledges etc but with the time the wheel changed the map of the world with thousands of inventions in the field of transportation and industries such as automotives and auto mobiles to transport different goods and people from one place to another. in olden manner the wheel was used to make different types of carts carried by different animals as bullock, horse and elephants etc. and these systems are continue in its original forms but a rectified way of the use of wheel has been in many purposes.

In this way, whatever the method would have been for the origin of life, the living body would have dependent on surrounding's nutritional elements, so these were "Heterotrophs". But due to this there would have been lacking of nutrients in the surroundings because of more consumption and less production. So only those living bodies would have remained which could achieve the nutrients.

Later on when these prepared nutrients exhausted, some other nutrients were being utilized after some chemical changes. So there would have been a certain type of selection by the nature of the living beings which could adapt themselves and became capable of utilizing these optional nutrients. In this way, according to the environment and availability of nutrients; varieties after varieties of the living creatures started developing in this environment.

Any of the living being requires energy to finalize any function or vital activity. This energy can be received by various methods such as fermentation, photosynthesis and respiration etc., where fermentation is a primary and easy system of getting energy in the living beings where some molecules of carbohydrates, The process of photosynthesis is a tremendous system of nature invented with time where the energy coming from sun is trapped and converted into tiny molecules like carbohydrates, fats and proteins; essential for a living structure. And then respiration is a process which gives energy by oxidizing these nutritional molecules obtained by the living creature, to finalize the living activities.

In this struggle for nutrition; the living beings adapted various methods such as parasitism, predates, saprotropism etc., the living creatures got nutrients from any of the way. But for how long this type of heterotrotropism would have supported the living world because one day all the nutrients and hosts would have exhausted. But then the invention of photosynthesis process in some living beings brought revolution in the living world, which gave a new range of nutritional elements for the living creatures and liberated oxygen which was *helpful to give more energy by respiration on place of fermentation and so on a new way of evolution was opened in life.*

In this way the nutrition has been the basic thing for the physical appearance and source of energy. So it can be placed as the first necessity of any living being. Even from a unicellular organism to the great extent of varieties, the nutrition is the source of energy for any creature which gives efficiency for a function. So this was one of the modes of physical aim of life in the sense of nutrition. Actually this is not only the Aim of life or living body but has been the first necessity for a living being.

2 Protection:—To maintain and keep living itself—

The second part of the physical mode as an aim or target of a living being is to keep it living and save itself from the surrounding atmosphere and the other species and natural disaster type events. It is very important factor for a living being to save and maintain its body. Any creature whether it is a unicellular organism or any huge or dangerous animal or a big plant; it has to prevent its body from its enemies and to keep existing itself. Although the animals and other creatures are not capable to built habitats but are forced to migrate and search the favorable habitat for survival.

Here living means to have a physical appearance and to have a specialty and also means to have capability to judge good and bad, required-non required elements, sense and various adaptations. Even when the life began as in the form of a micro organization there was the first necessity to keep existing and protect itself with the changing surrounding circumstances of the nature. So the living creatures started identifying the favors and started selecting the required molecules to get energy to maintain its appearance. We see each of the living being around us acts to protect itself from the enemies and from the inverted climate such as too cool and too hot climatic conditions. For this, each of the creature got much more adaptations and migrations from one place to another from time to time. As the number of the living creatures increased with millions of years the competition arose for the basic organic matter as nutrition and the struggle for the existence rectified and the creatures started identifying their enemies and they got the sense organs and the nervous system etc. The nervous system is basically adapted in this connection for protection of the living body. There are various types of systems and networks in the body of the living being for the maintenance and the existence for the living being itself.

In this connection there are various adaptations in the living creatures; for example if a tree is cut down totally but if the root is still inside the earth surface, the tree will grow up again; so this adaptation is for the existence of the creature. Another example is there that if a starfish (an oceanic water delicate creature) is cut down in many parts then each of the part will capable of creating a new creature; same as this the earthworm we see around us is also capable of creating the same creatures in some limited range if fragments are made of. Sense organs developed with the time are also for this purpose that the living creature could save itself from its inverted and unfavorable environment and also from their enemies. "Ensyphalization" in advanced creatures is one of the examples of the necessity of protection; Sephalization means that the concentration of the sense organs in the important part of the body through which the creature could understand the condition of the climate and the enemies by which it could be protected itself same as human has got all the five sense organs Eyes, Ears, Nose, Tongue and skin in its head. This is because the head will study the situations of the environment first then it will allow the body to go ahead. So this type of adaptation is to keep the body safe from the unfavorable environmental conditions and the predators.

Each living being has to struggle for the existence. In this regard it has to fight with its environment and the other animal species and also with the members of its own species. This struggle is for nutrition, for living with the physical existence and for their descendents. So in this way the creatures are in efforts to protect themselves and their descendents from the adverse of the natural circumstances.

3.—To reproduce; for the existence of the race—

When the life began on Earth the first unicellular organism started getting nutrients from the surrounding and kept itself in the existence; but later on as the situations became inverted, the task began for the existence and the unit started reproducing identical units as reproduction. It is quite clear that any living being has got a limited period for being alive because living bodies have to struggle with changing environment and adverse of the nature. *At the beginning reproduction was a very important* part of the struggle for the first living being. According to the definition of life that body is called living which gets nutrition, and has got physical existence with some vital activities and till this physical existence is fulfilled with the living conditions is so called living otherwise non-living or dead; but each living has to be defeated in the nature. That's why the reproduction is necessary for the existence of the race of a living creature.

Reproduction is the only thing which can give some new strength and new characters with some essential activities to fight with the inverted or changed circumstances of the nature. Starting from the beginning when the first living creature got split, it started multiplying and got the primary modes of reproduction such as division or fission etc. The living creature got existence and increased in numbers through this primary asexual mode of reproduction and produced millions of copies of itself and with the time some living beings started differing and became various species in millions of numbers. Reproduction is the only thing which has been the source of variability in living beings through adapting new characters and abilities to conquer the adverse circumstances of the nature. From micro and unicellular bacteria to largest living creature whale with billions of cells or whatever verities of living beings we see today are the results of this process of reproduction. Each of the creature reproduces to keep continue its generations and for the existence of the species and produces same copies of itself but in fact, each of the new produced copy or descendent is slight different from the generating creature but not totally same. This is because of the recombination of the genetic matter and the mutations occurred in the genetic sequence in expectations of some advanced abilities.

The first living being was a unicellular organism with primary necessary organelles and was in very small size about one billionth part of a meter; started re-producing same units as it and created many more units and showed the same vital activities. The reproduction became possible when the first molecule of DNA was introduced and it gave living phenomena to grow and multiply in numbers. Time passed, the environmental circumstances changed from time to time and from place to places and these living bodies reached to different places with different climate and different nutrients. The different adaptations were persuaded by some of these living bodies and developed up to different species. From time to time *these living beings changed into different races and developed up to tremendous verities of the living world and reproduction were the main source here for the variability in the nature. Through this process of Reproduction in generations of living beings initiated from the first living phenomena crossing about more than three billion years has got the millions of varieties of plants and millions of animal variety is seen here on this wonderful Earth.*

There have been various modes of reproduction in living beings. At beginning when life got split, it was necessary to keep exist the race and for this the process of reproduction initiated. As it is already discussed that any living being has required two basic needs for being alive; first nutrition and secondly to save the body and if any of these options is not satisfied then the question stands for the existence of entire race. So reproducing new units was one of the basic identifications for a living being. The living world started in oceanic water by unicellular prokaryotic micro organism and it was called 'Living' because of fulfilling these three basic characters. As life has prospered by the means of simple to the complex, same the reproduction process of the living creatures has also been from simple to the complex manner.

The first living beings acquired the simplest mode of reproduction, which was division or fission, in which a unit as a living being is divided into two or more parts and each part becomes a new living being same as the original one; same as the process of cloning. In this way, the first living being got a way to multiply in numbers and spread in different regions of the territory. Basically two modes of Reproduction are found in living beings; asexual and sexual. In asexual reproduction only one as the original unit can produce the descendent living being same as itself and as a form of same copies of it. When the first living being got existence, adapted this type of asexual reproduction where two gametes are not required and then the preliminary living beings initiated this type of reproduction. This asexual mode of reproduction was primary process for re-producing the same units of the simple and micro creatures and was helpful to multiply in numbers and spread over here and there, on every possible habitat opportune for the living phenomena. In asexual reproduction living beings produced just same copies of itself and multiplied in numbers but the only chance for evolution or adaptation was mutation in genetic consequence which is necessary to conquer the inverted circumstances. So the creatures reproduced through this asexual reproduction were not so capable to fight with the surrounding circumstances but the capacity of multiplying helped it to increase in numbers. Then with the time, these smallest living beings adapted some new modes of asexual reproduction such as fission, division, regeneration and budding etc. The micro and small creatures do have this type of simple mode of asexual reproduction; actually these creatures are preliminary and olden got birth as the initial living beings with the primary and simple systems of reproduction. These are in the same form and the reproductive system has been in the same form with many as thousands of generations crossed but remained in the original form without more changes in genes and having the existence even today, could be seen in micro different types of bacteria and other tiny aquatic creatures like amoeba, euglena, starfish and other small delicate creatures having no bone such as different mollusks etc.

Actually each of the creature born as a descendent of the original one as a copy of it, actually it is not the exact same as the original one but there is always a slight but un-noticeable changes occurs in genes of it to be transferred in the next generation, for example a living being gives birth to five descendents, each will be slight different from the original one due to the mutations appeared in the genetic consequence of the creature.

In this way, there are many advantages and disadvantages of the asexual reproduction. In this mode of reproduction a creature can reproduce a large amount of descendents and by this process the species is spread far around. This is for the existence of the race and to increase in number around the world. This asexual reproduction mode was the primary system of re-production of living beings but there are some limitations and disadvantages of this type of reproduction process and the descendents doesn't have quick adaptations against changing environment, no more variations and recombination are found in this type of reproduced units. All in all the asexual mode of reproduction has been opportunistic to the primary living beings for the spread to all over the globe and of course for the survival of the species.

Sexual reproduction—this is another mode of reproduction in advanced type of living beings. Any living being has to keep existing on the territory and also to conquer the changing circumstances for the existence; so the sexual mode of reproduction initiated where two gamete or living beings as male and female are there from different climates, give birth to the next generation followed with some new and advanced features. And this has been the only reason for the variations in living beings. It has been the cause of the large amount of varieties on this entire earth. There are two gametes as male and female for this type of reproduction. Here the recombination of the matter is done and a new range of varieties is generated.

In human being, this type of reproduction is found. This sexual reproduction is the only cause for the large amount of varieties of people found here. It is really a strange that there are about 6.50 billion people in the world but not any two of them are alike, it is due to this asexual reproduction, otherwise if there had been the asexual mode for reproduction in human; would have resulted the same copies of all the human beings no more changes would have occurred in the appearance of man and it is also suspicious that the race could have destroyed due to not adapting various abilities with the time in past.

In this way, we can finalize that the asexual reproduction has been helpful for the existence of the preliminary living organism species and the survival of those at the time of origin of life. And sexual reproduction in later living beings has been the shield for adaptations against the inverted climatic and nutritional conditions of the changing atmosphere; so these adaptations with time to time have been the cause for variations in the living beings with millions of years evolution and generated so large scale of varieties of the creatures we see today on the every possible bit of the globe. By the sexual reproduction creatures became more efficient from race to races to fulfill their essential vital activities as getting nutrition, protection and reproduction, to keep existing, successfully. In this long journey of millions years of sexual reproduction crossing millions of races from the primary living organisms acquiring a drastic change through the adaptations with time to time and species to species the most advance creature Human has taken place through the result of the sexual reproduction process of evolution.

The process of evolution takes thousands and millions of years to develop a species with a keen gradual variation in the characters of a living being whether anatomical or physiological. We can imagine how a long period of time was taken to create a living species into *other. A common view of human does not clarifies its origin because the evolution has given birth to the human in about 13 millions years from the old world monkeys with thousands of generations and thousands of adaptations in various physiological and anatomical characteristics with the time to conquer that time circumstances; all this happened to fulfill the basic requirements; nutrition, protection and reproduction to keep existing, as the aim of being a living being. So on after reproduction in races to races, the human was developed from a terrestrial small animal "Shrew"; initiating the primary primate characters, to today's advanced human being "Homo Sapience-Sapience", the modern man.*

8

Sexual Behavior

*W*hen we talk about the sexual behavior or about sex, attention simply goes towards the sex between a man and a woman. A man is attracted towards a woman and vise verse, each of the individual is attracted to the opposite sex; this happens with each of the individual un interrupted but reason unknown. Actually Sex is not only a state of mind but the body as well.

Sex is also one of the basic needs and the activity of a common man. Man is simply attracted towards the opposite sex because it is an autonomous and automatic system of activity. The human mind has various types of desires and feelings towards the opposite sex; to be having in touch etc but all these are because of the internal source of the body, which is

produced through various hormones and some other activities of the nervous system.

Man desires for various activities such as talking, kissing, hugging, loving etc and has got various emotions for the opposite sex but not just for the 'intercourse' because here in case of human, the mind plays a great roll in all the activities as well as of the body. Other creatures like animals act towards sex through various physical activities such as through smell or various types of sounds and of course through hormonal activities and also with climatic time periods. So this difference in human and other creatures is because the activities of animals and other creatures are resulted through feelings and in case of human the activities are result of thinking.

Human was also like animals which only could feel in the olden days when he was lived in jungles and no civilization was adapted. Gradually the time changed and mind developed up to millions of years and converted feelings in to thinking. As the man has been a social guy; as a father, a teacher, an employee and various `other emotional relations with the society, so the sex has been one out of one thousand needs of man but not the only one. So in modern Age all the feelings are filtered and altered in human mind and then served as the activities.

So we discussed that how a man is attracted towards a woman or the attraction of the opposite sex and also the sexual activities in other creatures and animals is found. But now it has to be discussed that why this sex has been launched? Why is it so?

Actually, in case of human or in any other animal the basic theme for the sex is to transport the 'Genetic fluid' from the male character towards the female and the basic thing here is to re combinate sperms; the male genetic matter with the Ovum; the female genetic matter, through which a new generation may be launched with new characters and activities and also with more ability to conquer the struggle for living in the new Horizon of the living world.

Sexual behavior is a great field, filled with a great deal of questions. **Basically, sexual behavior has been the recombination of the genetic matter of any living phenomenon as the source of variability. It is the story, begins; when the living beings got birth and started struggling in the nature. It is clear that when life began in water there was the question for the existence of the**

creature, firstly for the food and nourishment, as the definition of the word "life" says. Secondly, as the struggle began the question arose for the existence of the race too. For this it was necessary to re-produce, for the living being. Initially in those times life got birth in form of a quite tiny organism as a micro living cell; got various modes of reproduction as the primary modes of reproduction started such as division in the cell and resulted as a copy of the original one called the Asexual reproduction, where no two gametes or bodies required but one can produce the same copies of it.

It was the very beginning, when the life was not found here, when Earth was not so cool what it is today, when no imaginations could be imagined, when nowhere no one was lived, when the laws of the living world were not established, when no human civilization had taken place and when huge and enormous 'Dinosaurs' were not there to fight each other and were not jumping across the rivers and mountains. It was about 3.6 billion years ago when the story of the living world got split and which includes the coverage of the theme by which the sexual behavior may be watched out.

The definition of "life" tells that "the living being is so called; which can grow through various types of activities such as ingestion of food or nourishing substance and utilizing it for its growth and other vital necessary activities for protection of itself with the compulsion of reproduction". This word reproduction is a must to be rewarded as a living being. Here protection means to keep existing for being alive. This definition of life represents each and every creature whether a tiny or micro invisible living being such as a virus or bacteria up to the largest creature still known like a blue Whale having tons of weight means each of the race still born in the living world including us, the human being.

Reproduction means to produce the same units again, again and again; this is a basic character of any living being to reproduce. This process of reproduction takes the life from generation to generations and keeps continue the dramatic network from race to races. When life began on Earth it was necessary to re-produces and keep the race existing and so on the primary and olden modes for reproduction were adapted and initiated by the first living being.

In a broad way, we have extracted that there are two modes of reproduction sexual and asexual. In sexual reproduction two bodies or *living beings take part where the transfer, remixing or recombination of genetic matter is dong and then a new living being takes birth as a new generation same as their generating ancestors but with a new horizon with adapting some more abilities and beneficial characters entrusted from both of the parental living beings to get more efficiency to conquer the surroundings atmosphere and to keep existing itself and of coarse the race too.*

On the other hand there is another way for the reproduction called asexual, which is the primary and olden, the micro and primary living organisms are having this type of reproduction. In Asexual mode of reproduction only one living cell or organism may generate itself into one or some more new living beings as the same units of it. This asexual reproduction can be compared with 'Cloning'; which is a system of re-production from the common or somatic cells taken from any of the part of the body of any living being may generate a new living being same as a copy of the original one. In this type of reproduction, there are fewer chances for new adaptations and the creatures born as the next generation are less capable and weak to fight with changing atmosphere and the surroundings in the nature. The new units produced by cloning or asexual reproduction also carry the weak points or disadvantages like diseases etc in the same form as in the original one.

The Asexual mode of reproduction is the primary and olden one, was adapted and initiated by the first living organisms when the life got split. The primary living organisms such as viruses, bacteria and other unicellular organisms got this type of reproduction and yet living successfully in the atmosphere of the living world of today. From the beginning this type of asexual mode of reproduction developed up to various types according to the circumstances in last 3 and half billion years since the origin of the "life".

As it is clear that the first living being got existence in form of a unicellular organism and started re producing same units through this asexual system of reproduction where one cell or organism divides into two same parts and each part becomes a new living being same as the original one which may be called Binary fission. Today maximum of micro organisms do have this type of reproduction which was initiated at the time of the origin of life. And then after some million years and crossing thousands of generations in a monotonous form the living beings multiplied in numbers and a few of these living organisms got some mutations and converted into some other species and got some more characters and new modes for reproduction same as they adapted to get nutrition and protection with a huge period of thousands and millions of years. Then some more primary asexual types of reproduction were developed with time to time such as budding, regeneration etc. When the unicellular organisms became multi-cellular they adapted some new ways for reproduction as in budding; a living organism get developed a bud on its body which develops up to a new one same as the original one. And in regeneration if an organism gets divided due to any injury or some other reason then each piece becomes a new living being same as the original one for example Starfish found in the oceanic water, if it is cut or divided into two or more pieces each piece becomes a new living being same as the original one.

So the living beings at the origin adapted this asexual mode of reproduction which gave the simple and easy system of reproduction to fulfill the living world with wide spreading of the primary living races in all the possible areas opportunistic for the prosperity of the initial living beings.

At that time when the sexual mode for reproduction was still not invented in the nature, the asexual mode was the only source to save the living world to be continued. Thy asexual mode was very much responsible for the wide spreading of the life at all the possible area all over the Earth. As this asexual mode for reproduction was the primary system for reproduction for some million years initially after the origin of life. but there were some limitations for this asexual reproduction as it was not able to give strength to the living beings to fight the inverted environment of the nature because the re-produced units were as copies and same as the olden one, without more adaptations or changes.

Asexual reproduction was not so capable of creating variability and various modes for getting nutrition, protection and also for new ways for the reproduction and also some other vital activities. One more thing was there in asexual reproduction that the only chance for variability or adaptation was mutation (sudden changes in the genetic consequence; responsible for the structure and the activities of any living being).

In this way the asexual mode of reproduction was only capable for generating new units and could multiplied in numbers and also for the spreading of the living beings over here and there on the entire world.

But the creatures produced through the asexual reproduction were not capable to adapt some new ways for their basic needs such as nutrition, protection and to get some new vital activities and were not able to adapt some new modes to fulfill their requirements more effectively.

The asexual mode for reproduction was the only way for re producing living units initially up to about one billion years from the origin of the living era and the micro organisms like bacteria, millions of species of tiny creatures like algae and fungi and also many of the small creatures living in the oceanic aqua do have this type of asexual reproduction even today as these species are the direct branches of the primitive organisms having the simple constitution rather than today's so complicated world of living organisms.

As we saw that the asexual reproduction had been a simple and helpful for that time living beings but a primary system for reproduction which has its own merits and demerits. The merits of asexual reproduction tells about the wide spreading and the conquer in struggle for the existence of the race and various living species of the primitive eras of living beings and also was helpful to multiply in numbers through various ways of the re-production of the same units and kept the survival of the primary living species in the changing climate of the nature.

On the other hand, the demerits of the asexual reproduction show the incapability and imperfection to acquire new adaptations for the living beings on all the circumstances in the changing atmosphere of the globe. As it is clear that nothing is ideal and perfect and stable but the time and circumstances will change and to conquer these new circumstances the new mode for re-producing living units with some changes had to be launched as a new form of change. To get survival in the inverted climate conditions of the nature another way for reproduction was launched as sexual reproduction. It is not a miracle or a magic but it took millions of years and also millions of creatures with thousands of generations to get theses new ways and characters adapting in a keen gradual way called the "Evolution". This term Evolution may be clarified in further example of the development of various electronic devices for calculating mathematics such as an abacus, a calculator a personal computer as a desk-top a laptop or a palmtop; many other devices are there in our daily routine. If we see a laptop we find an intelligent convenient and too much complicated device with multiple calculations and much more memory, even comparing with human mind. Then we can imagine that how a miracle has occurred to launch so advanced device. But in fact it has been so with a great period of hundreds of years with a lot of inventions from time to time this is same as the Evolution occurred in various living beings. As we see all the devices which have taken place are present even today and are useful to us in various aspects and ways of our daily routine such as a calculator, an abacus a desktop and a laptop and even a palm top are available; same the Evolution may be explained where all the living beings got birth from time to time got various modes and characters and became various new species. And different species developed with different eras are present along with each other in the modern age of the living world same as many of the calculating devices existing such as a calculator, an abacus, a computer with their various variants; invented in different times and developed up to so advanced devices from simple to the complex manner and also having existence along with, in all the variants, in today's modern world of the information technology. Same in the process of evolution the huge amount of creatures is present invented from time to time.

Here we have to discuss the merits and demerits of asexual reproduction, where demerits which were responsible for the introduction of the SEXUAL Reproduction in the living beings.

Merits of Asexual reproduction—

ONLY ONE PRODUCER IS REQUIRED:—

This point of asexual reproduction tells the simple and primary way of the reproduction in the living beings. At the time of origin of life, this was the first way for re-producing new living units for the first imagined unit or a cell having life. There was no other gamete or body is required, only one living being can produce same units as living beings; so the first living units adapted this asexual mode of reproduction and produced new units by Fission and multiplied in numbers and then the life got step ahead.

ONLY ONE CAN PRODUCE MULTIPLE DESCENDENTS:—

This is one of the important characters of the asexual reproduction where one living body could produce many—more, in thousands new units by which the living creatures could spread in all over the areas of aquatic, terrestrial and aeronautic regions to find the favors for survival.

THE UNITS PRODUCED ARE JUST SAME AS THE ANSCESTER UNIT:—

The units produced in asexual reproduction are just same the generating unit and the basic theme of the living being is not disturbed.

HELPS THE LIVING BEINGS TO SPREAD VARIOUS PLACES ON THE EARTH:—

One unit produces millions of the same units and spread all the possible areas to get the vital circumstances to get the platform for the existence of the race.

Demerits of Asexual reproduction:—

NO FAST ADAPTING CAPACITY:—

Living units created by this mode get no fast adapting capacity against the changing atmosphere because the units produced in this mode are as a copy of the generating unit. There should be some capabilities to change itself, if the inverted or changed atmospheric circumstances occur to conquer the survival but the descendent units produced through this asexual reproduction have got quite less capacity of adaptations.

NO HEREDITARY RECOMBINATIONS OR VARIATIONS:—

This method has got no fusion of gametes (male and female genetic matter) so units produced as descendents have got no genetic recombination and variation. So on the asexual reproduction has been responsible for simple way where the race may only grow and multiply in numbers but can't produce variations or change.

FEW CHANCES FOR EVOLUTION AND DEVELOPMENT OF THE LIVING BEINGS:—

In asexual reproduction there were a few chances for Evolution and creating new species because the produced units were same as a copy of the original or generating unit. The only chance for change in the genetic consequence was mutation. The creatures are born just multiplying as copies of the original one.

In this way, the asexual mode of reproduction was quite efficient for the existence for the living beings and kept the living world continue through multiplying in numbers at the time of origin and provided opportunities to conquer the survival on all the possible atmosphere and became progressive for them. As the living world got split a long ago about 3.6 billion years, the living beings acquired this type of reproduction and started multiplied in numbers but a few could get survive and the rest were dead and disappeared. But those who got survival became the vector for the continuity of the living world. They developed up to millions of species in this period of 3.6 billion years and also continued in the same form and are present in today's atmosphere. All the tiny and micro organisms such as Viruses, different bacteria etc are present in the original form same as at the time of the origin and having this type of asexual reproduction.

As we examine the merits of asexual mode of reproduction it seems that when the life originated, the first need for the first living organization was; how to keep remaining itself? The solution for this came there to multiply and keep existing the race on spite of being a single unit. And so on this mode of reproduction in its simple form was invented by the first living being as the evidences have proved about 3.6 billion years ago. This asexual mode of reproduction was quote helpful for the existence and wide spreading the primary and micro organisms on all the possible areas on the globe.

But as it is clear that the means of nature is mobile, is to change, ups and downs, days and nights, rain and summer, hot and cool on its extreme; so there are many more points of view for the struggle for a living being. The demerits of the asexual mode of reproduction tells that the living beings created by this mode did not have more and fast capability against the atmospheric changes, creatures had no recombination and variations. So there was less probability of development and evolution. So a new way was launched in its laboratory for development, evolution and efficiency with capacity for fast adaptations to conquer the struggle in the new living Era in the form of sexual reproduction in its primary and simple form, in the primary and primitive micro living beings about 2.5 billion years ago after crossing one billion years from the origin and multiplying in millions of numbers but with a few changes through the asexual reproduction.

Millions of years near about 3600 (3.6 billions) have passed that the living beings have got the existence and there have been evolutionary steps for the development and increment of the varieties which has been possible only through the sexual behavior of the living beings for the process of re-production and to keep existing the race and races with lots of new adaptations and inventions in the anatomy and physiology of the living beings of different Eras developed in different regions of the globe with more possibilities to conquer the struggle for the existence.

There, in asexual reproduction the new units produced were in a simple way and as same, not same but just same as the old one. So there were less chances for the evolution by which it could fulfill its requirements; so the new way as sexual mode for the reproduction initiated in some micro organisms in a simple and primary manner, where the recombination of the genetic mater (DNA) was done in two same living beings called male and female; the two gametes.

As we know that always and everywhere the atmosphere and the climatic conditions are quite different and in a changing way, so some conditions are favorable and some are unfavorable, there are some regions also helping but somewhere it is inverted. So with the changing nature of the nature the living beings will also have to be changed to get success for the survival. And for this the invention of the SEXUAL BEHAVIOUR in some tiny and micro organisms, brought revolution in the field of variations to the living beings. All this happened beneath the sea surface because the life was still under the oceanic aqua it was the time about 2.5 billion years ago. All these ways of the evolutions have been proven by lots of discoveries and studies on a large amount of the living beings but in a common view we cant see and understand the process of the EVOLUTION because we were not the witness through all this process and as it is clear that how slow and gradual is the means of this process; what we can understand after seeing the period of 3.6 billion years of the living Era initiated.

As further in conclusion it may be said that when life began in the ocean it started struggling for the existence of its appearance. The struggle was to get energy to finalize its vital activities, because any of the activity or a work could only be done only through the ENERGY. And for this according to the definition of life the struggler had to act for the fulfillment of its three basic needs; NUTRITION, PROTECTION AND REPRODUCTION. And for these points of struggle the living creature has to have some devices; and these devices have to adapt themselves to overcome the in-favors in the surroundings. So on with millions of years of journey of the living Era the creatures have adapted themselves for getting nutrition, self protection and also for better rehabilitees in the nature, in a manner from simple to the complex and from small to the huge and the enormous physical appearance with the time as the largest creatures still known the DINOSAURS.

But this struggle for the existence is not the state for ones but it continues from generation to generations. In this struggle the asexual mode for reproduction has helped the creatures to remain the primary races surviving and has been helpful for wide spreading of various primitive species on various climates of the Earth which were originated after some sudden mutations. By asexual reproduction the species could increase in numbers but were not able to adapt themselves against various climates more effectively so the mortality of the descendent living beings born through the asexual reproduction was very high and most of the units produced were unable to survive. This is why the tiny and micro creatures produce hundreds and thousands descendent units; so that some of them could continue the survival and carry the dignity of the species forward. But this process of asexual reproduction unable to give more capabilities to the units produced as descendents through any more variation to conquer the survival. So a new way for reproducing new descendent units with some effective advantages of adaptations was invented and initiated by the nature with the time where recombination of genetic matter as male and female units of a living species could became possible in its primary stage which was responsible for variations and adaptations in the living creatures we see today on so large and scattered view of the modern conflicted and complex network of the living beings. The living beings born through sexual reproduction get more capability to adapt themselves in races to races and in each generation they *continue these new adaptations as characters and individuality and transfer them to the forthcoming descendent units in the next generation. So the living beings become more able to fulfill the central dogma of life, their basic needs Nutrition, Protection and Reproduction. And so on the life continues from one generation to another with the same dignity but also with slight difference to be stronger to fight the surrounding climate and creatures and conquer the survival and become the producer for the next more capable generation. As the studies have shown and the history of millions of years of the living world represent that the life has come to its today's so complex form from developing itself with the time and also through thousands and millions of generations after recombination of genetic matter. And this process of development has been from simple to the complex which has been possible just through the sexual behavior for reproduction. All the creatures we see through our common eye sight and of course ourselves the human being, do have this type of sexual reproduction, which has not been a miracle or a sudden appearance but has been so with millions of years crossing generations from simple to the complex and smallest or the micro organisms to the world of today's drastic range of varieties of the living creatures. Even the plants also have the sexual reproduction where the two genetic parts are within a plant itself as male and female present in the flower where the recombination is done through the pollination. We see the flowers of different plants are so colorful and filled with different nutritional substances, why is it so? It is due to attract the insects and other small creatures so that they help the plants by scattering the pollen grains (the male genetic matter) in the same flowers of the same types of plants but in different regions with different climates and nutritional availability. This all is for the re-combination of the genetic matter for more efficiency to conquer the survival of the next generation.*

In this way the sexual behavior has been a way and a basic need of any creature by which it could fulfill its central dogma of life. As in human beings, Man acts towards sexual behavior as his basic need and prominent activity but for the reason unknown as an automatic and internal source of activity. If we go in past when human was not a human but just a true beast. Human was same as the other animals do where the only needs were nutrition, protection and reproduction as a male and female. About human this story initiated about 13 million years ago when some of the old world monkeys and the early apes initiated towards bipedal movement and became the EARLY man. This early man lived in deep forests same as the other animals do with the common three basic needs nutrition protection and reproduction, crossed about more than 12 million years. Then 1 million years ago as the shape of a human being was acquired by the early man but the activities were same as the other animals do, they struggled for living in a way as an early man but with slight difference from the animals with the initiative characters of creativity such we see in some apes like; getting pulp and nutritional substances from any hard surfaced fruits as dry fruits etc by crushing them with stones, picking up the lice and some other harmful parasites from the hairs of the body. So these primary somewhat creative things went up to about850 to 900 thousand years and the useful characters which were acquired succeeded from generation to generations with some correction; all this happened just through the sexual re-production of the creature where the recombination of the genetic matter of different species made a slight difference from time to time and generation to generation to conquer the survival and originated different ancestor species of the human being, most of them lived in past and disappeared but the fittest living beings continued the survival and became the direct ancestors of mankind. Then about 100 to 150 thousand years back the early man became somewhat creative for its convenient, convenience for the fulfillment of the three basic needs for survival. And then the time changed and the early man initiated the proceeding towards the modernization, what we see today in the form of a rectified globalize society. And then man came to know the civilization by which it got a quite different status from animals. That was the time about 10000 BC when he came downwards to the field from trees and out of the jungles; started the social life and became a civilized beast. And the track way was from jungles to the society where man started utilizing its brain. This was the great revolution in the evolution of nature in which man started taming the world, on place of being tamed by the nature. When man an uncivilized creature there were only three basic needs; nutrition, protection and reproduction but even today as man has been a civilized being, he thinks before any of his activities but all his activities are centralized surround only these three basic needs because each of the creature is a traditional part of the struggle of the living world for the survival of itself and the species.

So we came to know that the human was just same as the other animals we see around us but then about ten thousand years ago when man got the brain as a result of evolution (the brain was evolved for creativity not as a miracle but in about past 130 thousand years) he started thinking; thinking about himself about his past his present and also about the future through which he had to fulfill his needs. He also thought for the convenience in the activities for which his attention went towards various techniques and artistic creation. Till then what the needs were now became goals to be achieved as he got the keyboard of the creativity for this the brain was so developed by the course of time. As human got bipedal locomotion the two fore arms became free to be called hands, became very much helpful for fulfillment of needs for living and then for the proper utilization of these two hands the brain went developed and more efficient with the time of about 130 thousand years. Through this man created society and true beast HOMO-SAPIENCE became "HOMO-SAPIENCE-SAPIENCE" the true human being.

So this change in the brain converted man from a beast to a civilized social human being and with these changes, his attitude towards sex also came to a civilized manner and it became he accepted monogamy (acceptance of one partner or married life etc) on place of polygamy (sex with multiple partners of the same kind same as the animals do) with the time and came to the track of uni-directed way on spite of un-directed with the life in society; utilizing the much developed brain by making it reason-minded.

Today when a human being simply as a boy or a girl or a male or a female is attracted towards opposite sex which is a quite natural phenomena because it is one of the basic activity of any living being which is for the re-production of new units as living of the same kind. This attraction between opposite sex may be understood through an example; we are using so many Almirahs and cup-boards to keep some things inside. A magnet is attached with the door of it along with an iron made plate in the opposite side and then we see the magnet is always attracted to the iron plate; so that the door is always kept closed by this attraction, we say it is the nature of magnet that it is always attracted to the iron. So this nature of attraction keeps the door closed as a common event but the basic thing which is fulfilled is to keep things inside the cup-board safe and covered, same in the sexual attraction the hormones are the magnet and this magnet keeps *attracted the opposite sexes but the basic goal which is obtained is to get the recombination of genetic matter between two generating units as male and female to get new living being with some more efficiency. But here an individual is involve in these activities as a common phenomenon but the reason unknown. As considering biology it is a physical activity controlled by various hormones in the body secreted by different glands. But actually this attraction is for a basic reason hidden in these activities which is for the recombination of the genetic matter through the male and female and to produce a new individual with some more abilities and more accumulated evolutional characters for more ability to survive and to continue the continuity of life.*

It is another thing that human has been quite different from the other animals and creatures because having much developed brain so he has got various emotions, feelings and relations in between and he can make various aspects for any thing also for the opposite partner another achievement for him has been that he may express his views or requirements by conversation and also through different artistic activities; so the view of the attraction in human being has been totally different in the form of a society and a family life but not just for the reproduction. In a common view the sexual activities of human looks like one out of one thousands but not the basic one.

So here nature gave him a simple and natural way to live as a common living being as a traditional part of the evolution but he changed it by altering it for his convenience and for better rehabilitations. But as we go on we will see that the basic behind all these activities is the central dogma of life surrounded by three basic needs nutrition, protection and reproduction because human has also been developed by crossing various steps from those simple micro creatures and animals. So there are so many common factors in the fundamental and elementary constitution of them. Also considering sexual behavior the theme behind the sexual behavior in human is reproduction same as the other animals do. But in animals and other creatures this activity is directed just through hormones as endocrine and exocrine in the body. In this way this phenomenon has totally automatic means in quite natural way. But in case of human it can be said as semi automatic as natural but artificially interfered by human mind. Here artificial is so called that an activity or work which is manipulated or finalized by mental inspiration. So the sexual behavior of human has been altered and converted by him for convenience and in its own way of expression in the form of a social and family life with different traditions developed in last few thousand years as the mentality enriched with much developed brain. Some of the examples of these traditions like man adopted monogamy (having one partner for lifetime after getting married) on place of multiple sex with many partners same as in animals. So many traditions have been developed by mankind and so the means of sexual behavior has been totally changed and two much rectified and different from the other animals.

As we see the animals have emotions just in the field of reproduction and for the descendent generations such as a female as a mother is attached with their infants and young successors until they become self dependent or matured but these emotions and feelings are for the existence of the race but considering human being he has got not only emotions like these but emotions for every thing such as relations with each other in various forms of the social relations, to identify good or bad, right or wrong, liking and disliking also various modes of expressions in between male and a female etc. So this field if thinking has been so wide due to the achievement of much advanced mentality to get convenient and comfortable life.

But if we go behind the activities of human as the social mankind, we will find the activities are surrounded by the only thing central dogma of life with the only three basic needs nutrition, protection and reproduction which has got the basic theme for the existence of any living phenomenon. This is because human is not apart from the other animals but he is basically a true beast. As we go further for the sexual behavior in human we will say human is quite different from the other animals, even human is human. This is because man has been a social and civilized guy. He has to follow the rules of the society, rules made by the society and for the benefits of the society; which includes the network of human beings as a part of it. If we check out the internal feelings of a human as a male or a female we will find the sexual interest towards each other is for multiple partners (as polygamy) which is same as in the animals. So man is not apart from the other animals and creatures but the activities are for the common and basic needs to keep existing and the survival with much—more abilities through the recombination by the sexual behavior. These internal feelings for attraction towards multiple partners are due to the law of natural selection where maximum numbers have to be born with slight differences through multiple recombinations in different living beings and the descendent units which are fittest; will continue the survival and rest will be disappeared. So this law inspires our internal feeling towards multiple sexes so that maximum varieties could be given birth and the continuity of the living world may be followed by the fittest descendent units born after the sexual recombination. But in case of human he has altered this means totally for his convenience by being a social guy.

Every creature except human acts in natural way of living but human has changed this natural way in his own way of living by altering it for his convenience. After all, in a concluding manner, human acts towards sex as his common activity which is automatically influenced from the internal source of the body as the natural fundament for keep living. We commonly act towards sex as a routine but the reason unknown. But actually this attraction towards the opposite sex has got the theme of the existence of the mankind and also has got the genetic consequence developed through the drama of past millions of years.

Till man was under care of nature totally, no civilization was adapted and when human had got the brain as just about four to six hundred cc engine (cranial capacity), he acted same as the other animals do and the concentration of this engine round the central dogma of life with just pre known three basic needs nutrition, protection and reproduction. So during this the sexual behavior of human was finalized in natural and common way by the hormonal and other physical activities. Man spent more than twelve million years in the natural way. It is another thing that now the scope of the activities of human have been so wide because this six hundred cc engine has now become about 1700 cc. If we go through the activities of human towards sexual behavior the way is too much expanded and rectified. For there are females having "Breasts"; which were just meant for "To feed" but now the definition has been changed, it has been a symbol for the sexual appearance in case of human being. Not only the breasts but whole the body has been the point of view for the sexual physical functions. All of these activities have been so diverted due to the appearance of the so much developed human mind because all the feelings and senses received through the sense organs are filtered and altered in the brain and then served as the activities of any kind. In the concluding manner there has been the way as "instructive" with the evolution of brain and it has been "constructive" with the two hands developed through the evolution to get the new horizons of the natural world.

So the human behavior towards all the living activities have been totally different also including sexual but all this has happened due to the influence of the brain developed in recent few thousand years nearly one hundred thousands. As human is not apart from the other animals all these phenomena are for the existence of the race. The theme behind the sexual behavior is to recombine the male and female genetic matter to get the new life and the new generation having new devices with more efficiency after mutations and changes in the genetic matter resulted in changed physical appearance with new abilities and characters.

So this is the natural and basic aspect behind the sexual behavior but here in the personal view of a person the sexual appearance is just attraction towards the opposite sex but for the reason unknown same as a magnet is attached in the door of a cup board to attract the iron plate but for some another reason, the goal to keep the cup board closed for the safety and cleanliness of the things kept inside. But there is enjoyment and excitement in a person for the sexual activities so he has to enjoy the life but there are various limitations because of being a social animal as a civilized and tamed; tamed by his own brain for his better convenience and for a globalize world's better society with beneficial interconnections. This all will be for the existence of the mankind which was in the natural way in past but now has been in its own way by the influence of the much developed human mind.

Love and other sentiments for the opposite sex is just the emotional aspect of human nature where both the male and female express various expressions and affections towards each other because of the mental influence developed in recent years near about 30 to 50 thousand years evolution. Whatever types of expressions and emotions are there in between, but the ultimate goal is for the sexual reproduction which is the foundation for the continuity of any living creature, of course the human civilization too. Here in case of human all the living and routine activities are finalized in the civilized and social manner and it looks quite different from the other living world but actually it is clear that man is not other than the animals even he has got today's modern form after crossing various steps from the ancestor generations of the animal kingdom being as a branch got appearance through the evolution in past 13million years. We see around us that the animals act towards sexual behavior through various expressions such as smell, sounds dancing etc it is due to the internal hormonal effect. But in case of human being man has got a very much developed brain as about seventeen hundred cc engine so all his activities are filtered and altered and then finalized through this brain even the hormonal activities for the physical external affairs too.

During the coarse of time and the development of mind, human has got a large amount of ways of expressions as development of various languages, various physical actions and face expressions, prosperity of literal means, development of so many symbols of love affection and hatred etc also so many artistic and mane made things have been developed in recent few thousand years. So the sexual activities have been diversified in its own kind, preferred in the social way on place of being a true beast by the modern human being for the better convenience.

After all these, the basic theme behind sexual behavior is to re produce a new generation of the mankind with much developed and more advanced abilities to conquer the living world through the accumulation of various required characters and physical appearance, where the sexual behavior makes a new recombination in each of the fertilization through the sexual activity. So the sexual behavior is an important and compulsory part of the living world where the basic thing behind the sexual behavior is the central dogma of life with the three fundamental needs; nutrition, protection and reproduction for the existence of any species even from the first living being as a single cell; the unit of life, up to today's modern animals and plants or the human being at the top most position in the "food cycle" of the living organisms.

The word "life" could be defined when the three basic needs were fulfilled in the first cell originated with the central dogma of life by the initiation of the protein synthesis process and began to replicate through "DNA Replication", means the life could be so called a living phenomena when it got reproduction. According to the evidences and the recent DNA study has proved that the life could get initiated about 3.6 billion years ago from today. This is why there are so many controversies among us about our appearance and also of the living world. And we were not the witness when the life began in the ocean because the modern man has just became modern and creative filled with the enthusiasm just 10000 years back from today and so on the creativity and understanding the nature could be initiated. There are so many evidences for the evolution of the living world such as the basic constitution of a living creature is same even a micro organism like a bacteria or a huge and the largest animal (A dinosaur or a whale even a human being) still found has got the basic structure made of the protein and the multiplying and replicating or reproduction of any living creature is just through the DNA with some what changes in each of the species. So the basic theme is same in all the living beings but the evolution has made many variations with the time for the success of a living being born in each of the birth to continue the existence and conquer the survival. So the sexual behavior has been the basic reason for the evolution and the variations of the living world in each of the recombination in each of the creature of a species. Human is not other than the animals and all the living creatures but the ways of expressions and the activities have been totally different which seems quite away from the other living world surround us.

The process of Evolution could be explained through the further example. We usually debate on a topic that 'What came first, Egg or the chicken'? Question is too much interesting, but no one surely answers this question because we were not the witness at the time of origin. We see a hen laying an egg and a chicken comes out of it after a certain period but we can't see the changes during the development of the chicken inside the egg. We do not know what and how do the sequences make a chicken developed. We can only watch a chicken becoming a matured Hen or a Cock. So in case of the question the answer either may be that the hen or the chicken came first to originate the egg. But here another question will arise 'Was there a miracle to introduce the chicken?

On the other hand we say the egg would have come first. We commonly know the egg very closely that what is inside it, a yellow yolk in the center surrounded by a colorless matter which is quite simple by our common eye. But how this simple constitution becomes living phenomena after a certain period:—THIS IS THE MIRACLE.

Actually the egg is a single cell which has got the hereditary consequence for the production and development of the chicken in which the central yellow part has got the nucleus filled with the chromosomes of the DNA with "genes" the basic mathematics of the generation and filled with proteins the main constituent for any living structure and so on the surrounding colorless part of the egg has got the carbohydrate or fats for the food supplements as the source of energy for the production process of the chicken.

The egg has got just a single cell the 'unit of life' whether the chicken has got millions of cells within it. Our common eyesight gives us the vision of the chicken as a single unit but actually it is a constitution of billions of cells generated from the original one out of the egg with the certain period for the hatching of the egg. So the egg has got certain pairs of DNA and filled with protein and fats. In spite of common eye the microscope, even the electronic microscopes developed with the time by the science has given the sight that how the single cell divides and one becomes two and two becomes four, four into eight and so on. In this way billions of cells develop and a unit as matured chicken is constructed to get birth out of the egg. The division of a cell became possible because of the DNA; the foundation of the living world. This DNA has got two basic qualities; first one that it can replicate and can create many copies of itself by which a new generation can be generated and a single cell unit can be multiplied in multi-cells and becomes a multi-cellular organism like the chicken.

Another quality of DNA is that it can create essential protein units by transcription from DNA to RNA, in which the RNA has got the copy with the codons as a base for the protein synthesis and so on these protein molecules in various forms create the body and structure of any living being. In this way the DNA was the first miracle to introduce the first living being with these two factors replication and transcription responsible for reproducing and making the structure of a living being respectively. No imaginations could be possible without DNA, from an invisible tiny or micro organism to a huge animal or a plant like a blue whale or an elephant even we the human beings because each of the cell present in any living phenomena is having the DNA molecules with the dramatic consequence of past generations to reconstruct a new copy of the ancestor generating unit to continue the pedigree of the species as the same. Without this DNA the definition of life could not be fulfilled where a living is so called which can grow and re produce a same unit; which is impossible without DNA having the codes assimilated within it for the copying and producing the protein for the structure of a living being.

So here we got that the egg is a single unit and a single cell with the signs of life and the chicken is also a single unit but many as billions of cells within it with the activities of life. How this single cell becomes billions? This is the miracle; and this miracle is due to the DNA present in the nucleus the yellow part of the egg which replicates and produces copies of the preliminary single cell and so the single cell is multiplied in billions in a certain period called the hatching period. Another thing that how this simple egg as a single cell makes the structure of a particular chicken why any other creature doesn't comes out of this particular egg? This is also due to the magical molecule DNA which makes particular structure through the transcription from DNA to RNA by creating small protein molecules by decoding the particular consequence of the ancestor living being as here the remixing of a cock and a hen. Here only the remixing of both the male and female is done for more efficiency but without any fundamental changes. The codes present in the DNA are responsible for the creation of particular organs of the chicken during the period of hatching in a gradual process.

In this way we see a single cell with more and more protein and carbohydrate in the egg produces a matured chicken by multiplying through cell-division and then from this chicken we commonly see the growing and the development of a hen or a cock. But we have never seen a hen or a cock appearing without this process or by any miracle. Only this process of the development from an egg towards a chicken and then a matured hen or a cock is the basic process for the appearance of a living species. This is the way where one cell becomes billions in numbers and gives a particular shape size and the specified individuality through the multiplying of genes assimilated in the DNA having the history of the past generation. The DNA, in the form of chromosomes, of a particular living being is having codes for all the activities and the physical appearance of the body and shape of the ancestor generation.

Here another question restricts that if the egg came first than there must be a hen to produce the egg, without a hen how an egg can be produced? Some other species laid some eggs and one of these eggs was with some mutations and converted into a chicken and the answer of this question is within the theme of the development of the egg and the production procedure of a matured chicken where a single cell becomes billions in numbers. Secrets hidden in the egg where a single cell becomes multi-cellular specialty has truly got the theme of the evolution and the descent of the living world. It means that the egg was the first thing which was as a descendent from some another species got some mutations and then got laid and gave birth to the chicken first time and so on the generations of the hen or cock got continuity of living.

So it can be said that the egg came first which was from some other species gave birth to the first chicken and created a new species due to the mutations occurred in the genes.

All this systematic evolution has occurred from species to species and generation to generation, beginning from one cell to multi-cells as the above explanation shows the development of a hen from the only single cell as the egg. As it is clear that the genes included in the DNA has got all the theme and all the activities and physical appearance of the generating living being in the forms of different codes so the same unit of the generating creature is produced after particular hatching period. We have known that millions of generations have been crossed in past 3600 million years after the initiation of the living being in the form of a single cell. And this single cell has become millions and millions of living species during the huge period of the evolution and the variations from species to species have occurred by the mutations (the sudden alterations in the genes or the DNA the basic framework of any living being which concludes new characters and also difference in the physical appearance) came to happen in the genetic consequence of the DNA of those different species from time to time and generation to generations and became responsible for the creation of different new species of the living beings. After each of the mutation the living being was acquiring some new characters and the accumulation of these mutations through different generations some of the descendent living beings were diverted towards another species and could became totally different from that of the ancestors of some generations back. The alterations in the genes are the result of remixing of the genetic matter and also because of climatic conditions as weather, food habits in the form of adaptations to conquer the struggle for the existence.

So the chicken has also been developed from any other species having sudden changes in the genes of the ancestor species, initiating as an egg which develops towards a matured chicken as we see as usual. So there was no hen to lay the first egg of the chicken but a female of some other bird species ovulated it and so on the new generations of the chicken were initiated and then the dramatic continuity of life went ahead as we see today commonly, the egg becomes chicken and this chicken is matured towards a hen or a cock then again a hen lying an egg. In the concluding manner, the egg came first to originate the first chicken from some other species due to the changes in the DNA consequences; having all the characters and individuality of the particular species. This development of the egg towards a chicken has got the theme of the development of all the living beings exist today where a simple constitution of the egg as a single cell becomes a multi cellular organism as a chicken with billions of cells, same there in the living world it has been proven by different evidences and different studies of the living creatures that the life had begun in the form of a single cell in about less than a nano-meter (1 billionth part of a meter in size)and as a simple constitution in the oceanic water about 3.6 billion years ago and developed up to millions of varieties with the time, even human is also the result of this so gradual process crossing thousands of generations in millions of years. The first cell was just a co incidence but through the re-production the drastic range of verities could get existence after conquering different climates and circumstances.

Another example of the process of our birth can explain that how a single cell having so tiny and micro body as about less than one billionth part of a meter in size becomes a huge body having kilos and tons in weight like an elephant and other living creatures including us. All of us have got birth from our mother and father and are having the mixed qualities of both of them; how it happens? We the human beings are living as a common man in the society and as a family in the common way fulfilling our routine and daily needs. An individual get birth as an infant as a small baby with about 3 kgs of weight which grows as a child then becomes a matured person with much more weight about 50 to hundred and above kilograms after a few years. This procedure is followed from generation to generation as in a common way and again an infant is born and grows up to a matured personality. Have we ever thought that how we are being born? The answer is simple that a person gets married with a lady and then a new baby could be born. We have made it convenient that *the system of marriage has been there for the sexual reproduction in the social way otherwise It was quite natural in the olden times same as the other animals do. The basic thing is that what happens after the marriage between the man as a male and a woman as a female that a new baby could get birth. Actually there happens the intercourse after copulation or mating where the male genetic matter in the form of tiny sperms having all the pro-forma and the total theme of the individuality as the DNA in the Chromosomes; enters into the female genetic organs where the remixing of the genetic matter is done through the DNA of the sperms and the ovum then a single cell is generated after the completion of the Chromosomes as the pairs which are ready to produce a new baby as a fetus in the womb. There are 110 to 200 million sperms in 1 ml of the semen ejaculated by the man where only one sperm get entered and fertilized with the ovum so we can imagine the size of an sperm or a cell and that how micro and tiny existence of this single cell less then one billionth part of a meter in size becomes a baby with about 3 kgs in weight and also becomes billions of cells within about 280 days of the pregnancy. In this way this period of 280 days can explain that how a single cell having too small as micro individuality becomes a multi-cellular organism with billions of cells and an individual personality. The DNA existing in each of the cell of an individual is having all the framework and story of the construction and activities of the recent generation in the form of codons concealed as the genes. These genes are the bases for any of the character and activity of an individual and also the individuality and personality as the body and shape of a person which are written in the DNA through different repetitions of four types of protein molecules. The DNA in the cell is always in pairs called the chromosomes; in case of a human being there are 23 pairs of chromosomes which are having all the individuality and theme of the structure, shape, size, height, and health, the color of the skin and also of the eye cornea etc. The chromosomes are always in pairs because each of us means the human being is re produced from two particular persons the mother and father. But in the genetic cells these pairs are separated and distinguished and becomes single strands of the chromosomes as in the form of sperms and the ovum in the male and female respectively to get fertilized from a new person as a male and a female from different regions and from different climates to recombined the genetic matter for the re production of the new generation to have some new abilities and efficiency to overcome the struggle for the survival in the new climate.*

Same in the evolution, the process of the development of so many creatures have been same like this process of the production process during the period of a pregnancy; it is also same in the production of a chicken during the hatching period of an egg. This production process of the living beings also explains the theme of the development of the entire living world where a simple single cell becomes a big or huge personality after multiplication in billions of numbers.

As all the living creatures we see around are looking quite different in shape body and many activities but giving birth or reproducing same units of their own ancestors and the descendents are as same as the generating one; this is because of the DNA present in the genetic matter with particular consequence copies of itself makes a new generation of its own. This is why a particular living being as a creature, an animal, a human being or a plant reproduces same units as the particular one. But the remixing of the genetic matter of the male and female through sexual behavior has been the basic cause for the initiation of different species of the living world with accumulation of different characters and abilities in the form of genetic codes inbuilt within the DNA found in the nucleus of each of the living being having the basic criteria of the particular species. This DNA is replicated and gives birth to the next generation of a particular species in as same as the original or the generating unit but the remixing of this DNA through male and female units makes a slight difference; so the new born unit as a living being is not just same but with some differences to achieve the efficiency and ability to win the circumstances found in the new atmosphere. So the birth of a chicken is also a result of this remixing of the DNA happened in the egg in many of the generations back and the procedure was from simple to the complex as from the egg to the chicken. Commonly we can't understand it easily because it is a keen gradual process occurred in millions of years to generate a species and we are not the witness for these millions of years, only the detailed study of hundreds of generations could explain the creation of so many species found in every possible area of the living world of this great BLUE PLANET.

Human status of social existence:—

The central dogma for living (The theme for being called a living being with the basic needs)—

A. food
B. Shelter or security
C. Descendent generation (reproduction)

Modern social status:—(Acquired by man in recent 10 thousand years for the convenience and to fulfill these basic needs in its own way by manipulating the natural world in artificial and the artistic manner through various inventions.)

1. Place
2. language
3. Emotional view
4. Family
5. Physical personality and Individuality
6. religion
7. entertainment
8. political networks
9. Fiscal interchange
10. Medicines and treatment

To be explained further in detail—

9

Human: Social Behavior

*T*oday we know the social status of human just as the common man. Man as a social guy, as a father, a teacher, an employee or student etc. lives in a common and simple way in the society. He has to fulfill his basic needs in form of daily requirements and routine activities. It has been so, by being reason minded for its convenience and to facilitate its own life.

It was not always from the beginning, as it is persuaded in the common way, but it has been the result of the evolutionary steps of the nature. It has already been discussed that how man got its appearance; which was through a gradual and natural evolutionary steps. This man got the existence after having life like other animals in the deep forests. But for a few thousand years this early man got the modern and social life through various cultural and scientific activities developed for its convenience. This was a sequent and gradual revolution.

It all began when not a definition or any identification could be given for the word life but there was the life as the struggling part of the ever-changing nature. So it had been launched out after a specific evolution and various revolutions from a few million years of Aquatic life to terrestrial life;. It is quite clear that man is not apart from the other animals and creatures but even basic and structural criteria are same there. So here man is just a milestone of the natural evolution but not the foundation stone; as it is considered in the social and common way. The difference here in human and other creatures is because of social and cultural development which is through the mind and the mental activities of the BRAIN.

It was about 63 million years ago when "Rock-Mountain revolution changed the MESOZOIC ERA into COENOZOIC ERA the latest era according to the geological time scale; the "Age of Mammals". There have been some great revolutions in the geography of the earth which have changed the climate and atmosphere of the earth in some million years duration which has been the reason for the great changes in the living world which resulted the decline of some dominating species and opportunities for the new species to come up and grow; same as the Fire makes a great change in the jungles and results the fulfilling the soil with nutrients and chances for new generations to grow with quit new characters and prosperity but on the other hand it destroys the old generations. This Revolution is so called Rock Mountain Revolution because in this Revolution some parts of earth surface and mountains went merged into the sea water and some merged ridges of the oceanic water came up and became the new mountains. This all happened due to the volcanic and earth quack activities of the hot magma flowing beneath the surface of the earth. During this Revolution; decline of Dinosaurs (the largest animals still known) and the other huge Reptilians was occurred and the new species with quite new characters the Mammals (animals feeding milk to their infants as supportive nutrients) began to develop. And through this sequence of evolution about 36 million years ago during the tertiary period of latest Era called CENOZOIC ERA (according to Geological time scale); monkeys and Apes began to appear in the deep forests. The monkeys and Apes went prospered up to about 25 million years and many species of them came into existence and lived in the deep forest for so many years. In this sequence many new species appeared and fulfilled their living, but *some species disappeared due to inverted climate and those which could conquer the new weather and circumstances continued their generations with some new characters adapted for the survival. In this consequence about 11 to 13 million years ago from today Man shaped Apes in the order of mammals began to grow up rapidly this period is known as MIOCENE EPOCH of the Cenozoic era. And so on about 13 million years ago from today the early man came to originate. This early man lived in jungles for a vast period of time about 12 million years struggling in its own way same as the other animals do, just for fulfillment of their three basic needs nutrition, protection, and reproduction just for living. So we can imagine that for how a long period, man spent in jungles as the early man living like animals and learnt some primary and initial activities. And then after a long period about 1 million years ago from today, this early man started thinking and it's became his by the social life towards modernization. The modernization: by starting utilizing of natural things for his convenience such as stones and bones for hunting, animal livestock for transporting etc. But all this was in deep jungles; still man had not developed houses and roads for the society but lived in caves and bunkers etc and still not invented cultivation. So there was the olden way towards social life because now the need for living safely and conveniently the togetherness and help to each other was required. This period of initiative learning some natural resources for convenience as in the olden way went up to about 0.99 million years (990 thousand years) also called the STONE AGE. It means today's human being could became totally modern just 10000 years back from today.*

So the early man, 13 million years earlier with the capacity of about 4 to 6 hundred cc (cubic centimeter) in it's skull to hold the comparatively small brain lived in natural way, not utilizing but using the natural resources. It was the time when natural evolution forced the pre man ape ancestors towards the early man according that time circumstances. At that time situation the tropical forests were destructed at a large scale; may be due to some natural disaster type events as fire, earthquake, volcanic magma, drought, or flood etc and big grass grounds took place; so the arboreal life of the early man was to be followed by terrestrial. Along with this they started carnivorous life due to lack of the big trees of fruits and other favorable vegetations. To get flesh they had to run on the grass grounds and for running they started bipedal movement. By this the two fore limbs were made free to be called "Hands" in spite of being legs. The brain with more developed "Cerebrum" (the most important part of the brain during the human evolution responsible for the advanced human activities) to control the all physical activities as autonomously. In this way Apes got down from the trees to big grass grounds and from fruit eating to flesh eating and became the new species as HOMO the early man. Initiating early man was same as the Apes do bigger eyes, dark and dense hairs on body, dangerous expressions on face but less active facial muscles, running fast on legs but much developed brain with some advanced activities than the Apes. It could be imagined that this early man struggled for how a long period of time about 12 million years and then about just about 1 million years ago he started some advanced and cultural activities towards modernization. Again it is clear that the appearance of human being has not been a miracle or magic but it is the result of millions of year's work of nature on the early species of early man. The period of 12 million years had been the most important period for the descent of man and then at the beginning of PLEISTOCENE EPOCH (the so called Stone Age) the early man started differing from the Apes least in physical but basically in mental and cultural activities. The Apes because of adapting erect posture with bipedal locomotion and two fore arms as hands were to be called another species Early Man. This process was basically held in Asia and nearer because more fossils of the linking species are found in China and Europe. The early man lived in forests in natural way same as the Apes crossed about 6 to 8 million years. About 4 million years ago the early man began to utilize the brain at a better scale and began to utilize the natural resources in it's own way such as stones, sticks and bones etc for protection then the new way towards the civilization initiated.

Then about 1 million years ago when the pre historic man began to use some things as arms and some useful utensils then to tame the emphatic utilization of hands the brain with more intelligence came to develop rapidly. This was the point which brought the early man towards the way of modernization. This was the time when the new species 'Homo' developed and the beginners of the human race as various pre historic species came and disappeared in different sequences; such as Java man, pecking man etc. Java man about 600 thousand years ago as the first true man with erect posture, cranial capacity about 1000 cc means a much developed brain lived in caves of Africa and China as omnivorous. Still they had invented fire and used stone arms for protection and hunting. And the Pecking man after 100 thousand years and about 500 thousand years back with more developed brain with about 1075 cc cranial capacity used fire at a better scale; started living in groups and were now identified with time and place. This was the time when the pre historic man thought the need of groups. This type of species spent up to about 300 thousand years and then about 200 thousand years back some new generations developed as the latest of human race; Homo Sapiens the modern man. These beginners of the species 'Homo Sapiens' struggled in nature's care and began to be socialized, this was because of much developed brain and these started thinking but couldn't be called modern disappeared about 150 thousand years back This species with a lot of members in the evolutionary consequences called 'Homo Erectus' because of adapting the erect posture still cranial capacity of brain was not more than 1100 cc. From this species the new species 'Homo Sapiens' the true and modern man with cranial capacity about 1450 cc began to exist about 150 thousand years back through the link wise many sub-species.

One of the sub-species of Homo named 'Homo-Sapience-Niederthelensis' lived in Europe about 150 thousand years back and lived up to about 115 thousand years and disappeared about 35000 years back. This was the sub-species which show the dominancy of cultural activities in the social way of living. The cranial cavity of these people was same as the modern man about 1450 cc. The brain had caught the super control on the overall activities of the body. This was the period when a lonely living animal deeper in the forests began to live in groups which was necessity of that time, became the convenience later on.

This was the sub-species which began to adapt sociality gradually by the course of thousands of years. Initially started living in caves in small families and began to identify 'my' and 'yours', then the rectified way of the struggle arose. An animal now came to be social, habit and habitat both had to be changed. Creative mentality had now been developed because of much developed brain with about 1450 cc cranial cavity; began to use arrow, knives etc, beautiful arms for hunting, prominently Rhino and Elephants. Animal skin was now used for covering themselves. These had now become quite social and division of labor had been at the social level. Those believed in religion and eternity of soul buried the dead bodies according their religion and traditions; but couldn't learn agriculture and animal husbandry. These were able to talk some usual sentences because of the development of 'voice'. These were the direct ancestors of the modern man but couldn't be called modern because of less developed brain. Due to the availability and abundance of trees with fruits and vegetations in the forests and preys for flesh; by being omnivorous they couldn't think for creative activities with interference to the nature such as agriculture and gardening etc.

This was the time when man had to come out for its own way of living and this was the story of the evolution for millions of years for the struggle to get the life of a 'Human being' from a 'beast' a journey towards a common man. The prominent feature for this evolution was the erect posture with two free Hands and a much more developed Brain. It is quite clear that the adaptation is a basic phenomenon for any living creature to overcome the inverted and difficult—situations of the nature. Adaptations in the living beings were in quite natural way at the beginning but in case of human he accepted the way for adaptations in its own way as social and creative for its convenience. To understand the adaptations we can go through an example of our usual life; here we see people of different skin color in different areas and several countries but we often think that why it is so? But actually it is due to the sunlight which affects the skin accordance with its sharpness and intensity. The tropical areas near the Equator are hot and the rays coming from the sun are sharp and more harmful to the skin and our body, so, to stop the effect of these harmful ultra-violet rays a pigment present in our skin cells called Melanin becomes condensed and helps to protect us from these harmful rays. As we go away from the Equator towards upward to North Pole or towards downward to the South Pole on the Globe we see less melanin in the skin and finally the skin color becomes lighter. Another thing in this connection, we see in the swimming, if we continue swimming for some days or months we see the skin color becomes darker of the skin which is directly exposed to the sun and the body parts which are covered with the costume remains lighter in color. This show the adaptation to save the parts under the skin from the sharp sun rays this is a little example of the adaptation as the protective to the body; there are many more activities as adaptations for the living beings *to overcome the struggle for the survival but we cant judge all these adaptations in a common way but all these activities are in progress in all the living beings in a hidden and gradual manner. The way of nature for the evolution is a keen gradual process but as the man got the key-board of its own life it got a very rapid way of the revolution in the life, not only of its own but all the nature from deep in the ocean to the eternal sky.*

About thousands of years back nearly 10000 men had got the social status at a better scale with a developed creative mentality to facilitate the life with the mutual conductance to each other and also for the whole community in stead of solitary living. The art of Agriculture, fishing, animal husbandry, etc. were now developed in a primary stage. And then the transportation on wheel was one of the most revolutionary inventions towards modernization. Use of fire was already learnt by men and now the food material began to be cooked on fire. Then this early man came out of the caves and began to create small huts and houses as they recognized the power of agriculture and so on they started living in groups. So these groups of families became the villages later on as the population increased. All these creative activities developed because of a very much developed brain with about 1650 to1700 cc cranial capacity in the Skull.

It is clear that today's status of human at so higher level of the society is the result of joint effort of people through various time periods. Various inventions with the time have made the life of man much convenient and more social. From the development of VOICE to the modern ways of the explanation through the most advanced Information Technology, human has overcome unfavours and got the ways to facilitate himself and his society. Here society represents an art of living together in a group or nearer with mutual conductance to help each other for comfort and facilities.

At the beginning when early man came to be called Human; a species separated from the other animal species, he was afraid of even the natural events because of least knowledge about the surroundings, so lived in groups and the enthusiasm appeared in the developing human mind and pointed towards creativity for convenience. Anyway by whichever method human came to be called MAN has got the apex position in the entire living world. In this way though human is appeared in his own individuality from those creatures but he has differentiated himself from those entirely by his activities in the social way through the most advanced MIND. However our social existence is the result of humans' activities to minimize the difficulties and inverted circumstances in the struggle for the existence and living conveniently by facilitating himself to fulfill the basic requirements and needs. Here we see different types of people, different ways of living, different habits, and also the different habitats, people with different personalities such as different types of skin color, different height health, different color of eye cornea, different food intake ; different people with different faces and face-cuts. All these differentiations are not the miracle or magic of a sudden moment or by someone but actually are the result of the experiments done by the nature on each of the personality during the creation in the womb through remixing of the genetic matter (chromosomes built with DNA) of mother and father and the adaptations acquired in the natural habitat for the existence. This existence is also the result of conquer of human being on difficult and inverted climate conditions, which is through the nature's law, Survival of the fittest as the natural selection; given by the great philosopher Charles Darwin. So this diversity in the individuality and personality is the result of recombination of the genetic matter of the male and female through the generations by which the species has conquered the survival.

It was the time when man came to understand the natural events as natural laws, natural phenomenon and the natural existence and got the ways for the co ordination with the nature and could become the most intelligent and successful creature of the wonderful blue planet. In this way, man has got the existence in the lap of nature as being a child; playing learning growing up with benign achievements and has become young through understanding the nature.

However, today we only know the human status as common and social as citizens in different countries living with not any particular intention but for the common and routine requirements as food, shelter and convenience etc. People with different languages, different clothing with different religions and cultures lives in different countries; even different states of a country, requires the same basic needs as nutrition and protection. Though all the human beings have separated from the same ancestors but have been differentiated because of differentiations in the habit and habitats and the surrounding circumstances of the atmosphere.

Present view of human existence defines the rectified spread and the proper investment of the brain developed up to so high level of the natural evolution. A well maintained and globalize society has been developed by the man for it's convenience through the link wise inventions in a gradual way but much faster than compared to the natural biological evolution with the time.

In fact we are a traditional part of the natural biological evolution in which the basic thing as the fundamental three basic needs are required for the existence; the existence not only for himself but for the race too; "nutrition" for getting energy to utilize for it's biological or living activities, secondly needs "protection" and security as favorable habitat in the climate and adaptations given by the nature and achieved by himself with the time to live safely and then the final and third need is "reproduction" for which they produce the same units as the descendent generation for the continuity of the race. Around these, are the basic activities of any living being, which show the struggle for the existence of the living world and various species? Any living-being existing on the planet acts just around these three basic things, any other activity beyond these intends towards just these three basic needs as supplementary. In this way these are the activities as basic for man in the struggle for the existence by which he represent the species conquered a space among all the living beings in the natural biological evolution. But through this evolution man has made a very much expanded, well co coordinated and too much convenient status as the social co-existence of the people in which the activities are so much rectified and advanced that the existence of man has been quite and completely different from the other living world. To minimize the struggle of the existence man has altered and given shape to the nature and so on to fulfill the basic needs he has converted the surrounding things and commodities into useful and favorable for it's own convenience and comfort. Through the dramatic network of the struggle in the nature for food, shelter and security of the descendents and of Corse for himself human has developed a much developed and more convenient society by the co existence of the people in course of thousands of years; in which man has discovered many more places and territory abandoned with the prosperity and quite supplementary for daily needs and requirements. To fulfill these three basic needs nutrition, protection and reproduction; man has altered his surroundings and developed many more things as his needs and requirements attached and included with human social living have become as basic and compulsory requirements. But in fact all these requirements and activities intend towards the three basic needs of any living being. These social requirements are prominent for human because human finalizes his all the activities in social way after filtration and alteration in mind. These social activities are finalized in the social way with the interchange and mutual conductance with themselves as the people of the society on spite of solitary living. So let's understand these social requirements and activities in present identity of man with help of various points:—

1. PLACE (Habitat):—{Presence on the territory}

It was the time when human started understanding nature, place and time; became reason minded but couldn't be defined as human, existing with the struggle for the basic requirements ; nourishment, safety and for the forthcoming race in wild and natural way. Today we see the presence of man on every bit of the land beyond water living systematically and successfully from American continent in the west, to Japan in East, from the distant regions of Siberia to distinct continent Australia; each of the landmass and territory has been favorable and opportune for human appearance. In common view this appearance seems to be present from beginning and people in different countries with different religions, different languages, different modes of food habits etc looks in its eternal form. But in fact, all these identities and activities have been developed with thousands of years. What the map of the world, we see today is political, which was but-natural before socialization of man and the basic structure of human existence is quite "Natural" but human has adapted himself and altered the Nature for his convenience in the form of society. At beginning man wandered from place to places in search of nourishment and also for favorable climate and of course for Water; the soul of life and any living activity.

To understand the existence on the territory, we will have to go back with the geological time scale; about 150 Thousand years ago when human was a lonely living animal wandering here and there for the preys. In those times human was under care of nature and where the favorable climate and conditions for food and shelter were available, he used to shift himself there. The living of man was same as the other animals do, but he started some activities as utilizing the natural resources for convenience and started living in groups.

There are various controversies among the scientists about the exact belonging with the place that where the descent of man was initialized towards modernization. But recent studies of DNA in generations of different people from different countries and some more evidences have shown that the evolution of man towards modernization was occurred in the great country Africa; the paradise for all the forthcoming and evolutionary species. Because of abundance of the vegetation and prosperity of nutrition and the energy in plenty from the straight rays of sun having the Ultra-Violet rays with more chances of mutations whether beneficial or lethal. Mutation is the basic event for evolution and development of any species. Mutation means sudden changes in genes which conclude the occurrence of new characters. These new characters help the creature to overcome the new circumstances of the surrounding Nature. With the development and accumulation of new characters a new species appears.

Nature's first law is Innovation; innovation to conquer the inverted and adverse conditions of surrounding atmosphere such as rain, lightening, hot rays of Sun having harmful and mutant ultra-violet rays etc, and also to chase with the struggle in inter and intra species as fighting with micro-organisms, Bacteria, Viruses, pathogenic Organisms and no doubt the animals and other enemies surrounding the living territory. This innovation gives strength to live successfully and fulfill the basic requirements; nourishment, safety and reproduction. The innovation has been the basic phenomenon to spread over here and there on the territory to fulfill the basic needs. Water and nourishment are the first necessities of any living body and for these any living being can leave the territory of its own and can go in search for them. But for human as the studies have shown that this was the basic reason to change the place from time to time.

So human lived in natural way as the other animals do, for a long period of time about Twelve Million years until he got the explanation and understanding about the nature and the natural events happening around him. During this period the habitat was unstable and undefined. So the natural shelter was caves, natural bunkers and trees etc. Then as he came to understand natural events occurring surround him and also natural things with the usefulness and utility of them. Then he came to start making small huts with the help of wood, and leather along with some other flora and fauna products; obtained from plants and animals. Some of the examples of this type of living can be seen even today in different and distinct areas of the world; such as a tribal community lives in Extend regions of Eastern Siberia of the Russian Continent. These people are mostly dependent on the only animal Reindeer, because of the too much cool weather and no vegetation. Due to a thick covering on the Earth's surface with Snow they are unable to grow vegetation or any other type of food supplement. Even no oceanic creatures like fishes, Prawns etc are available because of too cool temperature. But these people of Siberia use to shift themselves from one place to another according the weather and the temperature. They use to make tents and temporary shelter from the leather of this animal Reindeer, get food by the flesh of it and the fat is used as oil after heating and the fat is also used to fire. The only transport for them is this animal. The leather of this animal Reindeer is used to cover themselves and bones of it for making Arms etc. This animal Reindeer migrates itself from place to places with the weather. In this way, Siberian Tribal people are one of the examples of living in the olden age, living in extreme circumstances even in the modern age; on the other hand where man has got the keyboard of all the activities of his surroundings on his fingertips.

The common view of human existence looks like that it has been same from the origin and it is in its eternal form but now the studies of generations have proven that human was same as the other animals do but just about 10 thousand years back he could became totally modern through utilizing the natural resources systematically till then the habitat and place was unstable. Descent of man initiated about 13 million years back from the old world monkeys as the early Apes towards the Early man by the four pedal locomotion towards bipedal and then crossing generations in millions with adapting some new characters from generation to generation the early man lived deeper in the jungles same as the monkeys and other animal species fulfilling his basic needs for keep living; the nutrition, protection and reproduction crossed about 12 million years, still the place for shelter was unstable. Then about 150 thousand years back the early man got the initiation of the brain towards the development of mind and the mental activities. This mind gave him more ability to understand the nature and the activities for his convenience to fulfill his requirements in his own way. This was the time when he cane down from the trees to the plane grass grounds and started living in groups and used to hunt the animals in groups systematically. About 80 to 90 thousand years back the arms from bones and stone were initiated in the primary way for hunting. Then about 35 thousand years back the invention of fire could became possible through the much developed brain and then after some more thousand years later the introduction of wheel was the great invention for the revolution for the convenience as the transportation, still the habitat for the early man was the caves and natural bunkers which was about 20 to 35 thousand years back from today. Till then human as the early man had invented many more preliminary things for the convenience but couldn't be called totally modern. Then about 10 thousand years back from today when man could alter the natural things in his own way and initiated animal husbandry and could learn to grow crops and some other vegetation. So the life of man now changed totally when he could understand the importance of Land and became stable to be involved in the agriculture in spite of being a rover. This was the time when human could became totally modern and now the new way of the struggle initiated through understanding my and yours. The land according to its utility and of course the fertility became the reason for the stability of human being. This land also became the reason for different fights and wars from time to time during recent history of ten thousand years. Then the small families living in natural shelters as caves, bunkers etc now started making small huts with the help of the surrounding flora and fauna products. These small families became the Villages later on as the population increased. It means it is clear that the modern man could understand the nature and the natural things systematically and started making it convenient for his living with comfort just 10 thousand years back.

The recent studies of the DNA explains that most of the people as the human beings existing today are developed from the same ancestors about 50 thousand years back and spread in all the possible regions favorable for living initiated from Africa. It happened in the Age of ice when all the continents were conjoint with the ice. Today we see different people from different regions and countries with their particular individuality and personality. All have accepted their own territory and place for living in a common for the fulfillment of their needs for living in a social and systematic way, all this is in the modern way looks quite different from the other living world but actually it is also for the fulfillment the three basic needs ;nutrition, protection and re-production. Such as we have houses, clothing etc for protection, different food items in thousands of numbers, we are having children the descendent generation; all these are different ways adopted by the modern man but the basic goal is same as the other animals do.

In this way place, the living territory of human being could became stable just 10 thousand years back and the small families became villages and then these villages could be called cities later on as the population increased and when the systematic society could became possible by the division of labor then the initiation of different empires could become possible with the time during recent 5-6 thousand years back. And then the history what we could know through the invention of the modes of written literature became the evidences of our systematic and social living in the form of different political countries developed with the time. Various inventions in different fields made the life of human being much convenient and comfortable and gave the modern view of the society.

2. Language:—

We the human beings are quite different from all the other living creatures in so many ways, even it looks that we are totally different from the other living world because no other living being or creature has got creativity at so higher level such as building a drastic range of houses, having too much advanced information technology so many ways for entertainment, so much advanced system of treatment, total understanding about the utilization of the natural energy and also the great achievement of mutual understanding through the oral and also the written systems of language.

Yet, it has been proved that the human has got his today's existence in millions of years developing from the ancestor species of the early apes crossing thousands of generations and being a branch with the accumulation of different characters and physical appearance. In this connection the two basic things came to happen as revolutionary in the descent of man in about last 1 million years that the erect posture with bipedal locomotion and the other was the evolution of BRAIN. The second thing brain has been rapidly developed in last a few thousand years where the early man with bipedal locomotion started differing from the other living world least in physical but basically in mental activities and appearance. The rapid increase in brain was for the emphatic utilization of hands which were now free for the creativity and interference to the nature for his convenience. This rapid increase in brain came to happen in last a few thousand years nearly 100 to 150 which was quite fast in compared to other biological evolution When a species called Homo Sapience Nienderthalansis with much developed brain about 1450 cc space in the skull could get the appearance with more cultural activities and started living in groups and making small families. This was not a miracle but was the result of the natures work and experiments done on each of the new born descendent in thousands of generations in millions of species which came and disappeared from time to time and the new born became the victims to suffer the struggle for the existence and only a few could survive which were capable to fight with the natures different adverse climates. This all happened as a result of the natural selection of the nature where the most efficient and capable will survive and will continue the ancestor generating unit with the accumulation of beneficial activities and abilities. So we are also the witness for the conquer on the struggle in past and also the vectors of the abilities and characters achieved in last millions of years, the evolution of brain has also been the achievement of past generations given us as the entrust to get more efficiency. The detailed study of brain has clarified that the frontal part of brain called cerebrum has been the most important for the development of the creativity and other mental activities during the evolution of human from the early man in last 100 thousand years as so many evidences and fossils found by the scientists in recent years clarifies.

The development of Language is also one of the mental activities of the brain developed in last a few thousand years nearly 50 to 100, in a gradual way. It was the time when the need of living in groups influenced the human mind to identify my and yours, understanding the useful and useless things made the circumstances for the initiation of the primary voice. There were Neanderthals a species of early man with much developed mind about 1450 cc skull initiated much more creative activities such as stones and bones for hunting, animal skin *for covering themselves, use of fire at a better scale also believed in religion and buried the dead bodies and the eternity of soul and also started using some symbolical voice and some usual sentences. The initiation of language has not been suddenly but the period of thousands of years spent to develop so many languages in different regions of different countries.*

Today's common view about the language gives a drastic range of different languages. Were these present here as eternal? We see, there are more than hundred languages in our country itself, all are having there own identity and manner and have been developed from time to time and region to region as the population increased. As we know that the early man lived in jungles in the natural way not utilizing but using the natural resources same as the other animals do when the population was also in some limited numbers and when he was struggling for the survival by fulfilling the three basic needs nutrition, protection and the reproduction but as the population increased and the early man started making groups and the division of labor was reached at a better scale, the need of mutual interchange things and thoughts enforced the early man to make the voice and some usual sentences.

Actually the vocal cords present in our system for making voice are not only in humans but so many other living creatures surround us are having it, also the ancestor species as the early man did have these vocal cords present in the larynx but the development of brain makes the difference here where the overall control on all the activities of human are finalized after the alteration and filtration through the human mind developed at so higher level during recent few thousand years, where the most important part of brain the Cerebrum developed recently, has been the basic controller of all the modern activities developed such as various emotions, culture, creativity and relations etc. Language is also one of these advanced activities as the result of the evolution of the brain.

As we have learnt that man was a lonely living animal a long ago, started living nearer and also in groups and started making families. There were so many things now to be done through the mutual conductance such as hunting a big animal and using different arms effectively, and also making huts and bunkers; they started some symbolical language by making different voices which was definitely the result of the much developed brain. This symbolical language then converted in some usual sentences. All this happened about 30 to 50 thousand years back from today. This man with the initial system of language lived up to more then 20 to 30 thousand years in a simple manner not utilizing but using the natural resources and was dependent on the surrounding territory for the nutrition such as fruits, vegetation and the preys for flesh; so the hunting for flesh was one of the basic reasons to divide the work among different members of the group forced them to make some understanding with each other for better success. Till then man did not interfere the nature and couldn't learn animal husbandry and agriculture or gardening etc due to the abundance of preys and vegetation in the surroundings. It was the time about 10to 15 thousands years back from today, still the language was as in the symbolic and simple form; now started prospering with much more sentences and symbols through different languages in different regions of the different countries we see today. The much developed brain gave the capacity to convert the feelings into thinking and then this early man came to differ totally from the other living world and the 'it' became 'he' and then this thinking went to be served as the primary voice among various members of the group of the early man. The most developed mind made the difference to finalize the mutual activities among that time people.

Then human was using the natural resources and natural things for fulfilling his basic needs; nutrition, protection and reproduction in just the natural way but with some of his creativity which was also in the natural system such as stone, bones and wood sticks for hunting, living in caves and natural bunkers and also on the trees and also having the primary system of the language for mutual activities. As already the different descendent generations of the same ancestors who became capable to initiate the primary manner of language had now distributed in different regions of the earth during the Ice age about 40 to 50 thousand years back as the DNA study has shown in the recent years of the different people living in different countries and different continents. With the primary system of language the same people distributed from time to time and from region to region in search of favorable climate and also for the nutrition became the ancestors of different people living with different languages in so many countries in the present identity.

The initiation of noun is the first thing where the early man started giving names to each of the thing, place or an event for the convenient of his daily and routine activities as the capacity of the memory increased in the developing human mind. It was the time about 10 thousand BC means 10 to 12 thousand years ago man could learn the initial systematic language. This was due to the stability of life of that time people because of understanding the art of agriculture and making small huts near the rivers and other resources which were available and also where the fertile land was, also learnt animal husbandry through which they invented the transportation and also get various flora and fauna products such as milk to drink and fecal waste of cattle animals for burning etc. So this stable living on one place gave them to start a social life and when they got the primary languages to talk each other, so many systems got invented for the convenience and comfort through the mutual conductance and by understanding the feelings and thinking of each other. This understanding through the language made the systematic life of the human as a much convenient society and man could became a man on spite of being a beast of jungles.

Man has got memory much more then the other animals but with the course of time when he became social and came to understand the basic mathematics for living, the need of writing came to happen in the social life of human being. So the first systems of writing a few usual letters were now initiated near about 5 to 6 thousand years back, definably not more than that. And then as the first system of literal language initiated, the revolution occurred in the field of keeping the memorization and accumulation of documents. So the map we see today of the world is quite social and globalize which is just through the invention of the languages as in its oral and literal forms.

LINGUAL DISPARITY:—

We see that there are hundreds of languages spread in so many countries used by different people from different countries and different regions. There is a particular language of a specific region in a country also. How these languages came to appear? Were these present from the eternity?

No, actually we the people of different countries and different regions of the globe have got the appearance from the same ancestors a long ago may be from the Neanderthals lived here about 35000 to 150000 years back and have been distributed in several parts of various countries of the world. And those early people had invented the primary systems of the language as in the form of different symbols and simple words according to their convenience. Then accordance with the circumstances they were forced to shift themselves from time to time and place to place for the fulfillment of their basic needs. And so on the different descendant generations of them lived in different regions of the world as the branches of the pedigree from time to time. These people of different regions started giving names to the things surrounding them as the developing mind got different ways and much memory, also started making sentences as their own which became a different language of their own. So this happened in different regions of the world and so on so many languages got appearance. In different regions which were initiated from the same ancestors and same system of the initialization of the primary language.

In this way, all the human beings spread in all over the world have taken place from the same ancestor species, who had got the vocal parts to create the initial system of voice. This was the result of much developed brain especially cerebrum the frontal part responsible for the advanced activities of man, that he could make some primary words. There is no proper and exact belonging of the time that when this early man initiated the first words but it is clear that about 30 to 40 thousand years back these ancestors of human used to talk some usual sentences.

The modern network of man in different regions with different languages and religions shows a very much complicated view of the society. There are more than hundred languages been talked in different states and different regions in our country? How did these appear? It was the time when man got understanding about cultivation and growing crops, started living a stable life and also initiated small huts and houses for their families. To get the favorable habitat such as fertile land, availability of water and other resources, small groups of some families initiated living near different water resources such as rivers, lakes, ponds etc, for the basic thing for any living activity, the WATER.

These small groups of families initiated the simple but systematic means of language. Then as the population increased a particular language developed with the time for the convenience and mutual activities as being social. This process repeated in different regions of a country and also in different countries of the world and then so many languages developed and prospered with the time after initiating from the noun; by giving names to all the surrounding things. From time to time with the increase in population the migration of different people also made a difference to generate many new languages as branches adopting by different people in their own. We see a slight difference of region gives a quite different view of the language which is because of a separation of hundreds of years resulted as a quite new language with the use of new wordings generated their own. As we know that the population of different countries and states was quite less and there were a few people lived near various rivers and other convenient regions abundant with various resources a few thousand years back. So as the population increased they became a separate community according to their lingual dignity and became a separate state or area with a particular name and culture.

It was about 10 thousand years back when the human could became totally modern and also became capable to use different modes of languages and created a much developed society in form of small villages, converted in to big cities later. All this happened through the development of the language which made the mutual understanding better and the division of work more effective to facilitate the society with much convenience.

As the people started living in groups, mutual exchange of different things and material also started in primary way; not only things but ideas and thinking also began to be shared among them. Now the individual living diverted towards a social way and the need of mutual understanding intended the humans to initiate the conversation through symbols and in primary manner, all this was continue among them about 10 thousand years back. But as they started accumulating the animal livestock and other useful things surround them, the need of mathematics forced them to begin the symbols in written manner. And then the primary system of written language initiated according to the need. The brain was the most important thing in all these progresses towards the prosperity of various inventions.

These people of early times about 10 thousand years back spent about 5 thousand years with some changes in the written language not allot but about 5 thousand years ago from today when the systematic literal language could be invented in primary system of writing brought a revolution in the field of memorizing and helping man to keep the new things and inventions and also the events in s written language to be transferred in further generations. Then various mythological and mysterious books could be written now such as Bible, Koran, and Ramayana Mahabharata etc. There are so many books which are helpful for mankind in different ways such as the old granthas of Ayurved etc.

All the mythological books are maximum 5 thousand years old, not more than that because there are evidences of the oldest society in much civilized manner but which disappeared a long ago was the Indus Valley and Hardpan where a systematic and civilized manner was adapted for living in a social way. What the evidences have found, show that they used metallic along with earthen pots for making food, built systematic bath areas separate for men and women, used to burry the dead bodies, many social and mutual activities were developed such as a systematic drainage of waste water and small roads beside their houses but no evidences are found as in written language. So as no other civilization has been found out older to this, explains the disability of systematic writing of that time people. Then this systematic writing of different languages made a great impact on the people of a particular region and created new communities following the systematic written literature in the particular books of various myths.

So it is clear that the modern man about 10 thousand years back had been able to alter his surroundings and the impact of brain was much more emphatic on all his activities for living but the language was learnt at the primary stage as just oral and symbolic with some usual sentences. This was the time when he could conquer his survival much effectively and the mutual activities and division of labor among them made the life much convenient. Till then the descendent generation of these people having the primary lingual voice had scattered in different parts of world. These small groups of people became different communities and societies as they learnt and developed different languages as their own, prospered from time to time and region to region. Later these small communities became big countries according to their region as the population increased and the mutual activities became a prospered society.

It was the great revolution in the field of accumulation of various events and memories of the inventions held from time to time, when man could develop the literal language. As far as I know that there *has been not more than 3 to 4 thousand years when the first words in written form could be invented because the written literature what we have known still is not older to this period. As far as it is concerned that the Indian language Sanskrit and Latin from olden America and the Greek from Greece are known as the most olden languages and what the written literature has been found is not more than this period of 3 to 4 thousand years, even so many basic words are interchanged among these languages from time to time. As far as Sanskrit the ancient language of India has been the mother of so many languages developed in various parts of our country due to the different people accepting different regions as their particular habitat with the prosperity of the culture of their own. Here I would like to discuss that there are so many words in English which have been taken from this language the oldest one Sanskrit such as 'paternal' and 'maternal', words of English are trans words of 'pitra' and 'matra' which means father and mother, same as there the initial words of math such as 'two' and 'three' are also taken from Sanskrit where 'Dwi' and 'tri' which were two and three respectively. The nomenclature of months of the calendars also one of the example of the interchange of words from different languages to each other which was developed during the rising and the prosperity of the great Roman Empire. When there were ten months in the calendars January, February, March, April, May, June, September, October, November and December. Where the last four month names are derived from the Sanskrit where Saptam means seventh in position, Octom is 'Aushtam' means eighth, 'Novem' is ninth and 'Decem' is 'Dasham' which means tenth. So these are collectively named as numbers according to position; 7th '8th '9th ' and 10th '. But later as some of the intellectual people got some inconvenience in the calendar they suggested that time ruler of the Rome who was Julius Seizure added one month with initials of his name; July. Again there was some disturbance with the calendar so later in the ruling time of another Roman Emperor Augustus one more month August was added to the calendar to adjust the calendar properly. So these were some of the examples which show the prosperity of language from time to time and interchange of different cultures which concluded the prosperity of today's foundation of the literal and oral language at so much developed and cultured society.*

3.—Human nature (behavior among the people): IMOTIONAL VIEW

Human being is a living being same as the other creatures of the world where he acts same as them for the basic needs. But he has been prospered with the great thing Intelligence which makes him quite different from the other living world least in physical but basically in mental and creative activities. All this social status has been achieved in recent few thousand years when man started understanding the need of collective efforts of each other for convenience and security. This was the time when he began to identify place things and also the individuals as giving names to them along with a particular relation where it was too much convenient to live successfully and as a community for help to each other. Here the human being lives in the society as a common man with a lot of relations, particular position and having a special status in the society according to his work or occupation. All this happened with the evolution of the development of the most important part of the brain called 'cerebrum' the frontal and about one third part of it in size which was developed rapidly during the descent of the early man in last few thousand years.

There are so many relations with each other in a family and with some particular and close people which are for the convenience and for the need of each other. All these relations could be generated when man thought for small families and initiated the marital life as the society could be generated. Still human was same as the other creatures and animals do that he used to fulfill his basic needs in the natural way but now his all activities were tamed by the mind which was the basic controller of all his activities. It was the time when man came to understand the surrounding circumstances and the art of producing various crops and other required things by the joint effort of people and through the division of labor for more productivity, the stability came to the life of common man and this division of work created a particular position and level among them and also generated particular relations for convenience.

As we have known that the activities of human are being altered and filtered in the mind and then after proper thinking served in some systematic manner with a lot of expressions and various emotions. So as in other creatures the feelings are resulted in activities but incase of human those are the result of thinking which are converted *from simple feelings due to so much developed brain. In this way all the relations and emotions we are having for our nears and dears, elders and younger are due to the human mind by prospering a so developed society for his convenience developed in recent few thousand years.*

There are so many ways for the emotions in human nature where one of the views of the attraction between the opposite sexes is also in a rectified manner. Generally we see a man and a woman or a girl or a boy are being attracted towards opposite sex as the age of maturity initiates; they are having lots of emotions and various feelings for the opposite sex. It is because of the mental influence of the mind by which the activities are served in some special manner. We are being attracted to the opposite sex but for the reason unknown but the basic theme here is also the same as there in the other animals do which intends towards the third and last basic theme of the survival of a species where the genetic matter has to be re-combined through the male and female by which a new generation could be launched out with more capabilities. So the emotions and other feelings are just different expressions of human beings which are served in so systematic manner by the human mind which is not seen in the other animals but the basic theme is same for the living and to conquer the survival.

Human has got so many ways for expression and explanation where he can show his view and feelings in different forms of language, face expression etc in the form of different relations among them such as a father a mother a friend, a son or a daughter etc. These are the result of last a few thousand years when man cam to know the utility of all his surrounding and understanding the need of each other and so on he gave different nouns as names to all the things, people, places, creatures for his convenience and so on a social network cam to the existence with the progress of creativity in the mind. In this connection there are two basic things in human life as the point of view of the emotions and relations; first is that the emotions and relations between opposite sex as the male and female as husband and wife which is in today's social manner where it has been a marital life as a family. As already has been clarified that human activities are served as a result of alteration and filtration in the mind after converting the feelings into thinking but actually the basics behind these emotions, relations and lots of feelings between male and female are the third basic need for living to reproduce and to continue the survival of a species as the central dogma for keep living of a pedigree which is same as in the other animals and creatures but it has been socialized by the human mind for his convenience.

Second thing is about the emotions and relations between a mother and a child where mother gives feeding and care for the new born until he becomes capable for self efficiency. These emotions are also the result of the biological hormonal effect secreted in the body of a mother during and after the birth acquired during the evolution of millions of years. The basic thing here is also the basic theme for the survival of a species where a mother has to give nutrition and protection till the younger becomes capable to conquer the surrounding circumstances and becomes capable to get nutrition and security and could get ahead the continuity of the generation. All the basic needs are same here as compared with the other living world but human mind has made it much convenient and converted the natural struggle of man into a systematic and social manner by developing different things, and devices invented from time to time has made the life much comfortable which looks quite apart from the other living world which is actually same in the basic theme 'The struggle for the survival'.

4. Family:—

We are living in a society, have families and keep relations with different people as members of a family and also relations with other people out of the family. This is because of our understanding about each of the person and all the surroundings. It seems that all this network of different families and society has been eternal and invented by the god for our convenience and we are just a part of this system of the society. All of us live in a family with parents, brothers, sisters and also with some other relations, where we have given names to the particular relation.

Actually, this dramatic and systematic network of the society in the form of a family has been developed with the time spent in last few thousand years to fulfill our basic needs and to make easier our living and to minimize the struggle for the existence, in spite of having a life of an animal. As we have known that man lived in jungles for how a long period of time about more than 12 million years as an Early man *and spent a life of a true beast same as the animals do. But as he came to understand the natural phenomena occurring around him and became capable of creating some things and initiated utilizing natural things with the development of brain, then the need of groups on place of solitary living forced him to create small groups. This happened about ten to twelve thousand years back from today when man had already learnt so many things such as stones and bone for hunting, living in caves, use of fire but life was still unstable. So then he understood the use of land and initiated growing crops and started taming the animals useful to them. Then this utility of things and art of agriculture motivated him towards a stable life and those small groups became Villages later as the population increased. The cultivation and Animal husbandry needed the division of labor and the development of initial language helped them in this, through mutual understanding. This understanding initiated the life towards much sociality and then in the sexual activities the changes also came in human mind to make life much comfortable and pleasant by initiating the marriage life by which the future of descendants and also of them could become much secure and comfortable. And this decision of making the marital life made the society totally social and gave names to all the relations we are having today. Before this marriage life man was same as the other animals do, where so many fights and struggle were there in the sexual activities and the dominant male could have mating with the females and the forthcoming generation of him only could get ahead as the law of natural selection explains, which was unpleasant and un-comfortable in the social manner and then the social and mutual understanding in the developing human mind made so many decisions for the comfortable living in the society and so on the family life could began. In this way what the society we see today was not from the beginning but has been created through the mutual understanding of the people by so much developed human mind to facilitate the life of man much convenient and the family is also one of those decisions of the olden times which is defiantly not more than 10 to 20 thousand years old.*

So it is clear that the living of human became more social and comfortable with the time when the groups converted into small families and the life became secure in present but in future as well and a proper care and creativity came in the life of human in the form of so many relations. Now the descendents and new born were more safe and with more chances to survive with more and more comfort and facilities. The making of families and initiation of marriage life generated a long chain of relations and the mutual activities for help to each other became possible and soon this need made a much convenient society.

5.—Physical personality and individuality:—

The appearance of human is not a miracle or a magic finalized in a sudden time or a special creation as an instant job done by God as it is considered in the common way. But in fact, it is the result of nature's work of millions of years done in the form of lots of experiments from time to time, also through millions of chances of lost and found and after getting rid of millions of living beings and thousands of species. The appearance of human is also a systematic result of natural biological evolution occurred in past millions of years.

There have been so many species developed in past 3.6 billion years after the initiation of the first living cell with the invention of the first DNA molecule. Then the evolution prospered towards different branches of the living creatures as millions of species got appearance with the surrounding circumstances of each of them and so on this process was in a consequence; from simple to the complex. And in this consequence thousands and millions of species came and disappeared. Rest of them which could conquer the survival kept the continuity of life by being as branches of them towards a new living species.

The human physical personality is also the result of this natural biological evolution where from the old world monkeys being as a branch losing so many generations may be thousands with the descent and decline of so many species being a branch of the pedigree, after crossing millions of years got the today's individuality.

Human being is same as the other animals do particularly being as a mammal with some special characters of them such as hairs on body, hot blooded animal, females having menstruation, males having testes developed to maintain particular temperature for sperm generation, female feeding milk to the new born same as the other mammal animals do, giving birth to the fetus on place of ovulating or giving eggs. So these are some basic characters which clarify the similarity of human with the other living creatures living around him of *the same class-mammalia. Man has got the same physical personality compared with the closer branches of his past but similar species such as Apes, Gorillas, chimpanzee, some kinds of monkeys but the basic difference here is the proper erect posture and walking on two legs and the development of brain at so higher level. Otherwise man is same as the other animals do; two eyes, two ears one nose, teeth somewhat same, head, having a stomach four limbs where two of them converted as hands and rest two accommodated for locomotion but the brain at so higher level has made a great difference in the living of man that he looks totally different from the other living world. So all the characteristics of any living being have got a particular reason, same in human beings all the abilities and activities, also the appearance of different things of the body have been developed through the keen gradual evolution occurred in past a few million years by the recombination and according to need of that particular organ of the body through the transition in thousands of generations. In this connection two things are going to be discussed here; one is the disappearance of tail another is the need of beard on the face of a male human being. Here as it is clear that the process of evolution is too slow that we can not judge with our common view but a detailed study of generations could only explain the theme of it such as we know that the earth moves revolves around it's axis; here the speed of this revolving is about 30 kilometers per minute and in 24 hours on the Equator it completes a round of about 40 thousand kilometers, we see it regularly that the sun finishes a day by a way from east to west but in a common way we can' understand the revolving of the earth with so much of speed, same in the evolution each of the individual have some differences in each of the birth but the accumulation of these changes makes a different cast tribe and then a quite different species. Any way we are to discuss the disappearance of the tail in the ancestor species of human through past generations. It was the time about 15 to 50 million years ago when a group of old world monkeys being as the ancestors of Apes and also the man, adopted the life of grass grounds in spite of living on a tree, so the generations of this separate group got some different living where the tail was not required for the balancing on the tree and for climbing up so it went disappeared with the time and through generations lived up to millions of years and became the new coding in the genetic consequence of* the new pedigree and continued the new characters and abilities to conquer the survival.

Each of us is an individual and unique, there is no one similar in all the features of the physical existence or the mental activities but all of us are from a same species with a particular individuality and specialty having an specific identity with a different personality through a particular face body and also with more and more differences; this is due to the recombination of the genetic matter during each of the fertilization; means through each of the production process of a fetus by which a new descendant with some particular characters as a result of the recombination of the genetic coding in the DNA of each of the mother and father is remixed in each of the birth comes to the new dawn in the horizon of the living world to be a part of the struggle and carry forward the basic theme of the pedigree. Here we can understand the genetic coding in the consequence of the DNA through an example of the memory of a micro chip; where we commonly see in the modern era of the technology that a micro chip has got so much memory expanded up to 16, 32, and more GB (Giga Bytes) which can store so many videos, songs, images, a lot of documents and also the programs to run a particular games and also of the operating system of a computer. It is a wonder that how these big videos and all these programs are stored in this so tiny chip? Is there a miracle? No, in fact, there are tiny bytes which are kept in a particular sequence to make a meaningful result as an image or a video according to the size of it multiplied in the numbers of the bytes. These tiny bytes are different energy levels of the electrons which are kept in the particular manner; give the special result and the accumulation of these energy levels, give a particular image or a video which are stored in the chip as the forms of particular coding in bytes as kilo, mega and Giza in numbers. Same in a living being each of us are the result of this genetic coding inbuilt in the tiny molecules of a DNA where the accumulation and repetition of four base pairs which result the particular structure of an individual through making the protein molecules in a particular manner. And so on this DNA is re—combined through the generations which results some small changes in each of us and a new person is born as same as his parents but with a slight difference due to an experiment accused on him with a hope of some more efficiency to conquer the survival and keep existing the pedigree.

6.—Religion:—

    We live in a society as a common member of it with a personal identity such as name, religion etc given by the family and the closed people related to us as nears and dears. All of us believe in God through different ways and with different manners of pray and worship. According to different traditions and belief so many kinds of communities and religions have been developed with the time. There are two fundamental bases for a particular identity and introduction of a common man being an individual part of the society in the today's rectified view; the religion and the occupation. Here the religion and the traditions surround us make a great influence on the activities and living of a human being to become a common man with a personal status in the society as a particular part to be pointed out, this is because the traditions and the people present at the time of birth of a human as being delivered in the world make the basic identity of him. So since the birth to the maturity, this man is under the care and touch of his parents and the community with the traditions what they follow have to be followed. This period of the initial 15 to 20 years of age has got the basic roll in the identity and traditions of a common man. Then second thing which gives a particular identity to a common man is the work, occupation, job or business what he applies in his life for living.

    So we got that the religion and traditions are surrounded around us since the birth and we follow the traditions and rules as the common and routine part of our living, without getting rid of the reason behind that. The names, clothing, praying, different festivals, religious ceremonies, different ways and manners are being followed by us as our identity given by our community in the society.

    All these activities are due to the developing human mind for his convenience to identify each of the individual and the division of work with the mutual conductance and the achievement of voice made a great difference in the living of a human being from the other living world. The development of brain in recent a few thousand years in the evolution of human pedigree gave a particular direction to facilitate and make much convenient his life through the alteration in his surrounding. Again we will have to go back with the time when man was under care of the nature and just initiated the social and group activities to fulfill his basic three needs nutrition, protection and reproduction which are the foundation of any living creature, about

10000 years back. This was the time when human initiated the first and primary system of agriculture and the development of voice and the need of division of the work influenced them to give a particular name to the place, man or a thing means the invention of noun was done at this time. Still man was not related to a particular community or religion but lived in small groups on different land areas growing crops and started using pets for their routine needs. It means man could get the stable life not more than 10000 years ago.

As the population increased people started different traditions and religious activities in their routine life and those were now followed by their descendent generations. Yet, they were not called different communities and religions but as the system of written literature could be developed, made a great influence on different groups. And now a large amount of people could follow this written literature and a particular region with particular written literature in its own and particular language started generating different communities in different parts of the world due to the isolation of the land areas with the natural belongings to the mountains and rivers and different oceans etc.

We live in the society with a particular religion, all these religions are the result of different religious books such as "Ramayana" "Bhagwat Geeta", "Bible", "Koran" constructed in the ancient time about 3 to 4 thousand years back. This time has been definitely not more than 5000 years back as the evidences have proved The oldest civilization found yet is the 'Mohan Jodro and Harappa' which was not older than 5 thousand years, all the other civilizations still found are later than this. At those times a small amount of people followed the traditions and rules written in these books in different regions of the world and as the population increased the number of people became larger in different countries with particular religions could get a particular name and identity.

So the birth of the religion is not older than the birth of a human being but even man has given birth to the religion for his convenience and the saturation of his mental desires and to overcome the fearsome circumstances. The initiation of religion and religious activities happened when man was under care of nature and was unidentified with the natural phenomenon surround him and as he was afraid of the natural disaster like phenomenon such as flood, lightening, draught, different diseases as endemic and epidemic. As we know that the earlier human as Neanderthals, Cro-Magnon, etc the tribes of early man about 20 to 35 thousand years back were capable to speech some usual sentences, used fire at a better scale, believed in eternity of soul and also berried the dead bodies according to their belief but could not initiate a particular religion or community, only the systematic literature which could be discovered in recent time about 3 to 4 thousand years back became the bases for initiation of a particular community or religion.

Again it has to be clarified that as the human mind caught the super control on all the activities of human being made a great revolution in the world and also in the life of himself too. So the brain became instructive and the two free hands became constructive during the descent of man in last few thousand years and the map of the world became totally political and communal on place of but-natural as it was before the civilization of the human community.

The initiation of written literature became the legislation for the people present at those times in a particular region or a country and the points written in these olden mythological books became the rules of the society to be followed. The reason behind this was that the population was quite less and there were so many confusions and misunderstandings about the natural happenings and man was unidentified with the surrounding things, places, natural phenomena etc. As the population increased the followers of a particular region or a country multiplied in numbers and became millions of people as a particular community. The heroes of these mythological books became so much popular that they were given the noun as the god even the activities of them became the passion to be followed by the common man. Actually, these heroes are the ideals for us. This is same as in the recent years some particular characters of different popular books have become heroes such as 'Sherlock Holmes' A character of the detective series written by Sir "Arthur cannon Dial", Another example is the 'Harry Potter' a hero of the Harry potter series written by Lady "JK Rolling", These heroes have been so much popular that it looks that these were the heroes in reality and are not a fiction and people are so much influenced by these heroes as legends.

In this way, in olden times the written literature has been the legislation for the culture of a particular community to be followed and became a particular society and country later on as the population increased. Actually these mythological books can be compared as a ray of light in the dark and became the way to be followed for the saturation of their fear and the desires for success in the future.

If we go back to find out the origin of Indian religions, we will see that India was a country following the Hinduism before the arrival of the foreign invaders as the rulers before past 2 thousand years. There were two basic mythological books RAMAYANA and BHAGWAT GEETA which were written by Walmiki and Veda Vyas respectively about 3 thousand years back; put a great impact on the intellectual and social living of that time people. These books were so systematic and compiled with the real belongings to various places that became the legendary and the basic milestone for the society. The exact belonging with the time is not clear yet but it is very much sure that these books were written not more than 3 to 4 thousand years back. There were four VEDAS written after that from time to time by some of the intellectual people and described so many ways and kinds for living a better and social life. The people of that time followed the rules written in these Vedas and these rules became the legislation for that time society. This was the time when people followed the written literature and became a particular community called the HINDUS by following the language HINDI.

So only the written literature can defy the past by being the evidence in a systematic way. Some other books written later have shown the history of that time circumstances of the society; "Chanakya Neeti" written by a person named Chanakya is also one of the basic book with so many rules to live a systematic life which was written about 320 B.C. means 2330 years back from today. This was the time when Alexander the great, one of the first invaders from the Muslim countries came to INDIA and so on the Muslim rulers started entering the country and another religion now connected to our country. Yet the people were distinguished by their belonging to the place and the language they used to speak but the religion which being followed from the ancient books was called Hinduism.

Before the invention of written literature people lived in small groups fulfilling their routine and basic needs. These small groups became villages later with the increase of population, as they started understanding the surrounding nature such as plants, animals, crops, water resources etc; with their benefits. This was the time about 10 to 4 thousand years back from today. Then a systematic society could be managed by choosing one person as a ruler or a king, out of the people in a particular village. These particular kingdoms of small villages became cities and countries later. So about 3 to 4 thousand years back the literature of different mythological books put a great impact on the society and different people living in different regions of the Globe followed the particular religion written in these mythological books; BHAGWAT GEETA, RAMAYANA, KORAN, BIBLE etc according to the tongue being used as oral and written in their routine life.

So a religion is our theme and particular identity to become a unique part of the society. Each of us should follow the ideal rules of our religion, not by just copying but by understanding it and adopting it in our living to live a better and globalize society with the respect to all the religions existing in any part of the world. Basically each of us has got the existence from the same ancestors, thousands and millions of years back but with the time, we have adapted different religions in different regions of particular areas for our convenience.

We are too much superstitious and having blind faith in the religion, following so many rules in our day by day life but without understanding the reason behind it. It is because of the less understanding about the nature and the surrounding circumstances. It makes us dogmatic, fanatic and also conservative. In fact, the religion is a basis for our fundamental identity and the connectivity with a particular region and also gives a particular name to us. So the ideals and rules given by our religion should be practiced after understanding them and for the prosperity of the mankind in the modern identity and form of globalize and prospered society conquered the struggle of the past millions of years. In this way it is clear that man has got his social status with so much expanded back ground of various religions, different languages and different countries; scattered all over the world, has been developed in just last 10 thousand years before that human lived the life of a beast in the jungles for about 12 to 13 million years before the civilization.

7. ENTERTAINEMENT—

To understand the modern view of the social appearance of man, we should also go through the other curricular activities in our daily life such as different ways of entertainment between and among the *people of the society as some of the group activities. As we already know that man has got a total civilized and systematic society not more than 5 thousand years back as the evidences of some of the different oldest civilizations like 'Mohenjo-Daro and Harappa' tell us. There are so many ways for the entertainment in today's living of man in the form of different group activities and systematic manner like playing so many games. All these games are developed with the time in recent few hundreds of years with the time to time inventions. All this happened due to understanding the nature by the human mind through applying it for the convenience and satisfying himself other than the basic needs.*

As soon as human came to understand the nature and got the stability and also learnt the art of agriculture, gardening etc and started growing different types of crops and vegetations; the basic task for the nutrition was about to be solved by some of the groups of the people in some regions of the globe and now they could think for some other creative and entertaining activities in their routine life. This was the time when the need of groups became the convenience later on and small families in the form of some primary villages could be appeared. And soon as they solved the basic thing nutrition for their living, they could think for some new inventions for entertainment in the form of different games. As these generations had got a much developed brain scattered in different regions of the world and initiated their own manner for living and fulfilling the basic three needs for living and started group activities for their entertainment and amusement as now the basic needs were not remained basic but were the secondary. All these advanced creative activities of human are not more than 1o thousand years older because the evidences have clarified the artistic and creative living of man could initiate just after getting the stability through growing crops and making small huts for living and the division of labor also brought revolution in the social living of human being.

It was the time when man was under care of nature totally, lived like other animals and creatures in the deep jungles fulfilling his basic three needs nutrition, protection and reproduction for the continuity of life and the concentration was towards these basic needs to conquer the survival and to win the battle for the existence. There was no chance for the entertainment and amusement due to the unknown fear about the surrounding circumstances like natural calamities, other dangerous creatures which could be harmful to them, unstable place and territory. All this was due to less understanding about the nature and surrounding, so as man came to understand his climate and surrounding things and the other living world and also when he became creative and self depending for fulfilling his basic needs; the basic three needs became secondary and supplementary, then man could think for some other creative and entertaining activities. So the goal now became for the 'living' on spite of 'struggling'.

We see there are so many ways for the entertainment of man such as physical games and various equipments like a wide range of electronic devices have been developed for the entertainment in recent years which has made the life of man quite apart, totally social and systematic from the other living creatures. There were the natural systems for the entertainment before the revolution occurred in the field of electronic devices. It means the life of human has been totally different from the other living beings due to the intellectual prosperity, the basic three needs for living have been secondary and man has been quite apart from the other living being. But in fact, the basic theme is same there as the struggle for the existence; existence for not only himself but the generations of future.

8. Political Map Of The Society:—

It is quite clear that man is not apart from other living creatures but he also finalizes his all the activities in the theme of the central dogma for the victory on the struggle for the existence by fulfilling the basic three needs nutrition, protection and reproduction. But the way and manner has been quite different, in the modern view of the globalize society. There are so many continents, sub continents, countries, states, cities and different villages having their own identity and a particular name existing on every bit of the land mass with the possibilities of life.

The political map of the world we see today was not present from the beginning but, in fact, this is also a result of various time periods in past, about 10 thousand years back, initiated from the group activities and need of groups. It all began, when man could understand the nature and the surrounding natural things useful for him and the stability of habitat and understanding about cultivation and animal husbandry came to his life by which they could think for the accumulation of the natural useful property surrounding them like land for agriculture, source of water, animals and plants useful to them. Then to occupy these natural resources different groups started battle among them as the population increased. Then to get success, there was the need of a well planned system, group understanding and a better division of work, to be followed. So in this consequence and with the development of voice with the systematic languages a great system of work's division came to the existence where a person was chosen as the chief and others had to follow the instructions of the chief. Nearly all the villages now followed this system of social living and man was now civilized and became the true HUMAN BEING a common man, a well equipped and civilized part of the society.

These small villages became small towns and urban cities later as the population increased. Then the new way of the kingdoms came to appear as the chief of some villages started the invasion on the neighboring territory to capture the natural resources and property and then the battle for the kingdoms initiated. And so on different Kingdoms came into existence in different parts of the world, were given the names of their own. This system of kingdoms of the society is not older then 5 thousand years from today because no civilization as totally systematic is found earlier than the Indus-Valley civilization which is proven about 5 thousand years older, just after this any systematic society could be imagined. After this, so many kingdoms came and disappeared and then what happened in recent 2 thousand years we know very closely due to written literature of the history. So many kingdoms invaded on each other and ruled for different time periods on different countries but in the last 20th century the new way of ruling as the democracy brought the world in a view of a political map with more than 3 hundred countries ruled by the people, of the people and for the prosperity of the people with the new horizon for the life of each of the individual to live with convenience and comfort.

Last two thousand years have been very important for the globalization of the world, where so many systems for traveling and transporting could be developed and man from one country to another could reach easily and so on people could interchange various inventions and culture among them. In this connection here we can understand the globalization of the people and spreading them in the world through the example of Indian history. India was a country with its own and olden culture with the traditional living with using the *natural resources such as pet animals, olden systems of agriculture, no more means of transports etc before the foreign invaders came here. It was about 323 B.C. means just 2336 years back from today, when Alexander the great the first invader from out side the country came with the only means of transport; 'Horses'. Still no other system for traveling was invented faster to this. Till then there was no way to enter in our country, then some other invaders from the neighboring Islamic countries came to India and ruled for centuries. The mix up of different cultures could be possible and various inventions could become the foundation for development of the mankind and spread in the entire world. Till then there were small kingdoms and ruling systems in small villages developed as the group activities for the systematic society. India is a country which is almost covered from all the surface, where three sides are surrounded with the oceans and the upper surface is covered by the Himalayan range of mountains so it was about to be cut from the neighboring countries the only way to enter the country was from the upper eastern part which was connected by the land area of the Islamic Arabian countries like Iran, Iraq, Saudi Arabia, Afghanistan etc until the marine transport could be invented. That's why so many rulers such as Mughals etc Islamic rulers etc could enter our country due to no more means for transportation still invented. Other then these Islamic rulers the Portuguese, Dutch or British people could enter in our country in the 15 century A.D. when the first European Vasco-De-Gama in 1498 A.D. Discovered India for the outside world. It means India was still in its traditional living with less developed equipments such as arms of olden system, cooking on natural products obtained from surrounding flora and fauna and was also divided into different small riyasats and talukas means small social kingdoms ruled in different small regions of the country.*

Today we live in a society where a globalize world with more than three hundred near about 350 countries being ruled and managed with the political system for the people developed from time to time. There are more than 6.5 billion people living in different countries fulfilling their basic needs and routine activities following their own cultures developed in the past from time to time for their convenience are called different citizens according to their belongings with the territory of the region of a particular country. Human mind has been able to understand his surrounding nature and has altered and given names to all the things he need and also what he invents with the time and also has been able to understand the nature and the natural things with its laws and has been able to alter and manipulate these things in the consequence for the usefulness and the utility with so many discoveries and inventions finalized in past few centuries.

9:—Fiscal Interchange—

Today's modern view of the human social status shows a well planned and systematic monitory way of the interchange among them where a need or a necessity in the routine life is fulfilled through a mutual exchange with the money. Here a job, a service or any thing; useful for a person is being provided by a particular standard or price may, also be called the value is being fulfilled by the money. We can say the money is the blood of the society which provides all the things, services or matter to any part of the society same as the blood do within the body.

The modern view seems to be that this monitory system of exchange or interchange among the people is eternal and it has been from the origin of the mankind. But actually it has originated when man came to think of the group living and this group activities enforced him to make understanding between each other and the requirement for food, shelter and security initiated the primary system of interchange things such as food material, division of the work for hunting prey or for doing cultivation and then distributing the product obtained from this group activity initiated the mutual exchange among them.

All these activities were the result of the much developed mind; which was now more specified with the time for proper utilization of the two free hands. It was the time when man started making some things for their need such as arms from bones and stones, pots as earthen, and later from the metal, also the pet animals useful to them and the usefulness of a land etc; so now he was to think these things as his property It would have been in the Stone Age about 7 to 8 thousand years back, not earlier then 10 thousand years from today. This mutual exchange of things converted in some metallic coins or metallic foils as man came to understand the nobility of the precious metals; the gold and silver as the appearance of the system as political came to existence in the form of different kingdoms to live *a systematic and secure life for the people of a particular community or a society in a specific region on the territory. It was the time about 4 to 5 thousand years earlier from today when the system of different kingdoms came to exist as the population increased then these kingdoms now started a new way of the struggle for men as the battle for acquiring the fertile, useful and beneficial land and property by becoming ambitious to obtain much more.*

This system of ruling a particular region or a country prospered up to more than 3 thousand years where the mutual interchange among the people was done through different ways as initiated from things such as cereals, food material, different metals, domestic and useful animals etc but later went up to the metallic coins initiating from precious to iron became as a particular currency of any kingdom or a country but in recent years about 2 or 3 centuries earlier in 18 th or 19 th century as the political countries came into existence. Now all the things useful for the common living, services and assets were now exchanged through a specific currency of a particular country.

In this way it is clear that as man caught the super control on all his body and came to understand the surrounding nature due to the so much developed brain the two free hands went constructive on so rectified manner for the modern living in the guidance and instructions of it. Today's view of our social living is so much expanded that we see different things being finalized in hundreds and thousands of specific manners where this fiscal interchange and monitory system to get any thing needed also has got so many kinds for exchange in modern times for example we see so many types of coins, note, Cheque, demand-drafts, even internet banking which is without any document transaction. So all these have happened in recent years as different inventions and discoveries have un-covered the secrets of the nature and the natural things surrounding us. So only a few centuries have been there that man could understand the social interchange through the currency which has too much simplified the living of a common man and made much convenient through providing so many services and things needed in the routine life. All this has been the result of group activities and social living of the modern man.

10 Medicines and Treatment:—

Again we have to go in the past when man initiated living in groups. When he was too much afraid of the natural events, all his surrounding nature and natural things which were unidentified to him but he initiated some social activities like hunting in groups, making some arms etc but couldn't think for more creativity. It was the time about 10 thousand years back when man could learn for some creativity at the primary stage such as making earthen pots, small huts and could learn the initial systems of agriculture and started keeping the useful pet animals. Before this time the life of man was full of struggle same as other animals do but as he could understand the utility of land for cultivation and gardening the life became totally stable. This stability opened so many ways for the creativity and efforts towards the modernity where the enthusiasm of human mind clarified the nature and natural events happening surround him and human could unfold the mysteries of the natural laws through the discoveries and inventions finalized from time to time. The invention of medicine has also been the result of these inventions due to the human eagerness for his better living.

Yet man was under the care of nature and lived in natural manner same as the other animals do. But he could be called totally modern not more than 10 thousand years earlier because there are the evidences of the Paleolithic and Mesolithic period of the human social living when he could become creative by making so many things useful to him where Paleolithic period is about 7 to 10 thousand years earlier as the evidences clarify and the Mesolithic period was followed to Paleolithic period which was about 5 thousand years earlier. But there are no evidences in these times for the use of any type of medicine.

We see that each of the creature acts to fulfill his three basic needs for living; nutrition, protection and reproduction but in case of human these needs are same but the way has been quite apart from the other living world due to the creativity of brain where the mind generates its own way and manner for all the activities. Man has been able to understand the surrounding circumstances of the nature and in this connection he also came to understand different diseases and ailments happening to the body, with the time. A systematic knowledge of the anatomy and physiology of the human body could be evaluated in recent years as the invention of written language could became the best media to transfer the knowledge from generation to generation. In the olden days man was afraid of natural calamities and the diseases and ailments were quite fearsome for him but as soon as he came to understand the reasons and the pathogenic organisms surround us he could invent different medicines and treatments to conquer the illness. Recent two centuries as 19th and 20th have been very important for the progress and prosperity of different medicines such as first antibiotics, antiseptics and anesthetic medicines have been discovered in these centuries which have been revolutionary in the field of medicine otherwise human was totally dependent on the natural support that's why people used to die in numbers before the invention of the primary antibiotics and different endemic and epidemic diseases were prevalent in those times.

As human got the much developed brain with the evolution of past few thousand years, he came to understand the Anatomy and physiology of the body and the recent inventions in the field of medicine made the life more secure and different treatment systems became possible to assist the struggle of the survival of mankind so the mortality rate decreased up to a great level and man could get success on different ailments. It all became possible by the much developed human mind which has been evolved in recent few thousand years and so on man could became creative in different sectors of the survival in the living world.

Conclusion

The above description of life is the basic theme of the living world where the living beings got the appearance and existence after a keen gradual evolution and passed near about 3.6 billion years where a micro and tiny single cell living-being having the existence of less than one billionth part of a meter in size got the appearance first in the deep ocean and made the possibility of the living world to go ahead. So the evolution from simple to the complex and from micro to the huge living creatures being as different branches in several Eras went ahead crossing millions of years and then about 13 million years back being as a branch, the creatures like human beings could began to appear and a new Era could be initiated and the new ways were opened for the appearance of a quite different creature from rest of the living animals and creatures the "Human being".

So the appearance of human being was not a miracle or a magic generated by the god in a sudden time but the pedigree of millions of generations made the circumstances for today's individuality of man. The only process for the generating or producing a human being is the sexual activity between a male and a female where the sexual intercourse makes the circumstances for the recombination of the genetic matter filled within the ova and sperms having the fifty percent means 23chromosomes in each to make the pair and initiate the process for the creation of a new human being. Here we know that there are about 200 million sperms in one milliliter semen of a male human and each of the sperm is having all the theme of the individual such as different characters like the skin color, the color of eye cornea, the height, health and the personality, also the face and the physical calculations and same, the ova of a female human being is having the same characteristics of herself but existing so tiny and micro in size. So we can imagine that how a tiny and micro organization of the sperm and ova becomes the generating unit of a new human being and develops up to a fetus having the mixed characteristics of the generating forefathers. Then we see this fetus get birth and grow in a new individual and continue the dramatic network of the living world. All the creatures we see in the world are born in the same way where an extreme small means micro egg or we can say a single cell having the theme of the generating pedigree as the male and female; produces a new generation after being recombined through the fertilization according to the chromosomes and the DNA existing in the ancestors transferred in the egg through the sperm and ova. This single cell after multiplication becomes a big and a particular living being with specific characters of the individual species inbuilt in the genes of the chromosomes. We see there are different types of plants of different vegetables and fruits such as lady's finger, bitter gut, spinach, orange, apple or a lemon etc in our daily life, each of them have some seeds within them and if we want to grow any of these vegetables then we will have to take the seed of the particular vegetable and to put in the soil and will have to give favorable circumstances such as water, fertilizers etc. and so on a particular vegetable can grow. Here it is to be noted that a lady's finger plant could only be grown by the seed of a lady's finger and a lemon plant by a lemon seed only. Why it happens so? And why does a lemon seed can not produce a lady's finger plant? In this way, a particular seed has got the basic theme and the individuality of the particular plant in the form of DNA concealed in the chromosomes in the seed; actually this seed is the single cell unit of this particular plant which will grow into a plant of that particular kind of the generating unit after multiplying in numbers and becoming a multi-cellular organism. Here a small seed has got the capacity to generate a new living phenomena of a particular species which means any of the living being has been developed from a small and simple structure to the complex creatures being different species from time to time after some changes in the genetic consequence of the DNA with different climates and circumstances resulted in to various living species of so many creatures and plants from a small bacteria to the huge dinosaurs and from a tiny Algae to a big tropical plant and whatever variety we know, all of these grow from a small and tiny seed or an egg of the particular kind of its own.

This process of the development of an individual also clarifies that all the existing living species have been developed from the simple and small creatures in a keen gradual period of about 3.6 billion years through the Evolution and have got the specialty according to different climates and habitats after conquering the struggle for the survival with achieving so many modes and systems of nourishment, safety and of course the different ways for the reproduction and kept the network of the species existing in the world.

In this way, we got that we are the traditional part of the natural biological evolution where man is just a milestone in the history of the creatures still born being as a branch but not the foundation of the living world, what it is considered in the modern circumstances. All the creatures, plants and whatever the living beings we see around of coarse including us are a successor part of the dramatic network of the natural biological evolution and also is a part for the experiment of the nature in the laboratory for keep existing with fulfilling the basic theme of being a living being; the Nutrition, protection and reproduction. All the living beings we see around have conquered the struggle of the surrounding atmosphere and got the existence of a particular species after crossing so many generations with a slight difference in each of the generation in past 3.6 billion years where some varieties of the living beings continued in the same identity and others changed from time to time and kept the pedigree continue and increased in numbers became a particular race or a species, so the verities we see around could get appearance at so huge amount by changing themselves to fulfill the basic needs for the survival.

There are so many controversies and confusions among the people about our existence and the surrounding living world of the nature. The above clarification would have justified the answer to the existence and appearance for our wonderful creation of the nature.